HMH Florida Science

FLORIDA STATEWIDE SCIENCE ASSESSMENT (FSSA) REVIEW AND PRACTICE

GRADE 8 STUDENT BOOKLET

Houghton Mifflin Harcourt™

Diagnostic Tests

Science Benchmark Reviews

FSSA Practice Test

Introduction

To the Student

This booklet is designed to help you prepare to take the Florida Statewide Science Assessment (FSSA). The table of contents at the beginning of this book shows how the book is organized. The first section of the book contains review material and practice questions that are grouped by topic. Following the review material and practice questions is a practice test. The practice test is followed by an answer sheet for recording your answers for the test.

When you take the FSSA, you will be tested on the designated Science Benchmarks. Each of the Benchmarks that you may be tested on is included in the review and practice section. Reading the short review of each concept, and then answering the practice questions that follow, will be a good way to check your understanding of the material.

Taking the practice test will also help you prepare for the FSSA. The practice test should be similar to the FSSA test that you will take. After taking the practice test, you may find that there are concepts you need to review further.

Test Taking Tips

General Tips

- Read the directions carefully before you begin.

- Budget your time based on the number and type of questions. Set aside time to recheck your answers after you're done.

- When using a separate answer sheet, use a ruler or blank sheet of paper as a guide to avoid marking answers on the wrong line.

- If there is no penalty for guessing, it's better to guess than to leave an answer blank.

- Guess well, not wildly. Try to eliminate one or two answer choices first.

- Read the question fully and carefully. Many students miss the correct answer because they read only part of the question, and choose an answer based on what they think the question is asking.

- In the question stem, note key terms that tell you what to look for in the answer choices:
  What? When? Where? What NOT? What kind? How many?

If you encounter a question about a key term or vocabulary term that is unfamiliar to you, try to break the word up into word parts. If you know what part of the word means, you may be able to eliminate some answer choices.

Using Images

Tables and Graphs

- Read the title.
- Note the units of measure.
- For tables, read row and column headings.
- For graphs, note the data points.
- For graphs, read the axes labels.
- Look for trends and patterns.

Diagrams

- Read the title and all labels.
- Do not rely on relative sizes of items to compare size. Look for a scale.
- BEFORE you look at the diagram, read the question all the way through. Look for hints in the question that will tell you what to look at in the diagram.
- AFTER reading the question, read and look through the whole diagram to understand what it illustrates, and what processes or parts are involved.
- Follow numbered steps in order or trace arrows to understand a process.
- Look at the diagram's parts and then see how they work together.

Maps

- Read the title, key, place names, and names of other map features.
- Note the scale, compass direction, and location of important features with respect to one another.

Using Reference Sheets

- Before beginning the test, look at the reference sheets to see what is included.
- During the test, when a question addresses a topic included on the reference sheet, look at the reference sheet after you read the question.

10 The graph below shows the number of people who visited doctors because of influenza-like illnesses over a two-year period

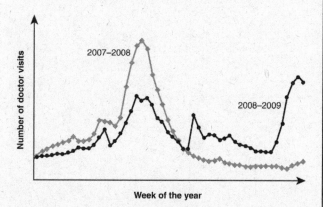

Week of the year

What can you conclude from this graph?

F Influenza-like illnesses follow a steady pattern throughout the year.

G Scientists can predict that the number of influenza-like illnesses will decrease for 2009–2010.

H The severity of influenza-like symptoms decreased in 2008–2009.

I The number of people who developed influenza-like illnesses did not peak at the same time in 2008–2009 as it did in 2007–2008.

Name _____ Date _____    **Nature of Science**

Nature of Science

Mark one answer for each question.

1 Ⓐ Ⓑ Ⓒ Ⓓ

2 Ⓕ Ⓖ Ⓗ Ⓘ

3 Ⓐ Ⓑ Ⓒ Ⓓ

4 Ⓕ Ⓖ Ⓗ Ⓘ

5 Ⓐ Ⓑ Ⓒ Ⓓ

6 Ⓕ Ⓖ Ⓗ Ⓘ

7 Ⓐ Ⓑ Ⓒ Ⓓ

8 Ⓕ Ⓖ Ⓗ Ⓘ

9 Ⓐ Ⓑ Ⓒ Ⓓ

10 Ⓕ Ⓖ Ⓗ Ⓘ

Earth and Space Science

DIRECTIONS

Read each question carefully. Determine the best answer to the question from the answer choices provided. Then fill in the answer on your answer sheet.

1 Which lists celestial bodies from largest to smallest?

    A asteroid, sun, planet, dwarf planet

    B sun, dwarf planet, planet, asteroid

    C sun, planet, asteroid, dwarf planet

    D sun, planet, dwarf planet, asteroid

2 The Venn diagram compares the composition of different types of celestial objects.

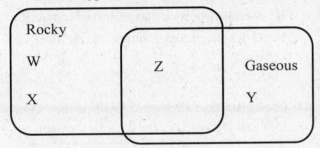

Which letter represents planets?

    F W

    G X

    H Y

    I Z

3 Which is used to determine a star's temperature?

    A color

    B composition

    C shape

    D size

4 Which describes why two stars of the same size might appear to be different sizes when viewing them from Earth?

    F A star's distance from Earth affects how small or large it appears.

    G A star's shape affects how small or large it appears.

    H Brighter stars appear larger than stars that are less bright.

    I Yellow stars appear larger than white stars.

5 A planet's surface gravity influences the thickness of the atmosphere that surrounds the planet. This table shows the surface gravities of the terrestrial planets as a percentage of the surface gravity of Earth.

Planet	Surface gravity (% of Earth's gravity)
Earth	100
Mars	37
Mercury	38
Venus	89

Based on their surface gravities, which terrestrial planets would have the thinnest atmospheres?

    A Mars and Venus

    B Earth and Venus

    C Mars and Mercury

    D Earth and Mercury

6 The table shows planets' distance from the sun in astronomical units (AU).

Planet	Distance
Mercury	0.39 AU
Venus	0.723 AU
Earth	1 AU

Which can be explained by the data shown in the table?

F Earth is cooler than Mercury.

G Earth is larger than Mercury.

H Earth is larger than Venus.

I Earth is warmer than Mercury.

7 The diagram depicts the positions of the moon, Earth, and sun.

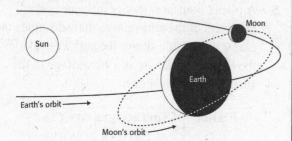

Which describes what happens during a solar eclipse?

A Earth blocks light from the sun from reaching the moon.

B Light from the sun shines more brightly.

C The moon blocks light from the sun from reaching Earth.

D The sun's light no longer reaches the moon.

8 Galileo Galilei discovered that the planet Venus had phases like the moon. Which provides evidence for Venus's phases?

F The sun orbits Venus.

G Venus has a moon like Earth.

H Venus orbits Earth.

I Venus orbits the sun.

9 Which results from the melting of rock deep within Earth's surface?

A drought

B earthquake

C tornado

D volcano

10 Granite forms when liquid magma slowly cools within Earth's crust. If the granite is exposed to intense heat and pressure, it can change to gneiss. Which change takes place when granite turns into gneiss?

F Sedimentary rock changes into igneous rock.

G Igneous rock changes into metamorphic rock.

H Metamorphic rock changes into igneous rock.

I Sedimentary rock changes into metamorphic rock.

11 Geologists have discovered fossils in the locations labeled 1, 2, and 3 on the diagram.

What can scientists infer about the age of the fossils?

A The fossils in locations 1 and 2 are the same age.

B The fossils in locations 2 and 3 are the same age.

C The fossils in location 3 are older than the fossils in location 1.

D The fossils in location 2 are younger than the fossils in location 1.

12 The diagram shows Earth's layers.

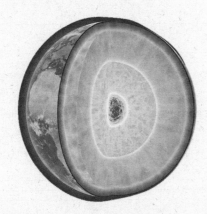

Which layer of Earth is composed of moving plates?

F   crust

G   inner core

H   mantle

I   outer core

13 Which results from plate tectonic activity in Earth's crust?

A   earthquakes

B   hurricanes

C   thunderstorms

D   tornadoes

14 The concepts of weather and climate are related but different. Which statement describes weather?

F   A thunderstorm is expected tomorrow evening.

G   The average temperature from 2000 to 2006 was 20°C.

H   The average yearly precipitation from 1998 to 2003 was 17 cm.

I   The sun shines for 300 days of the year in the area.

15 Humans burn fossil fuels for many purposes. Which describes one way that the burning of fossil fuels impacts Earth's atmosphere?

A   decreases the amount of carbon dioxide

B   increases the amount of carbon dioxide

C   increases the amount of nitrogen

D   increases the amount of oxygen

16 Heat energy is transferred through Earth's systems. These images show objects that transfer heat energy.

Electric heater   Hot plate   Convection oven   Fireplace

Which object uses conduction to transfer heat?

F   convection oven

G   electric heater

H   fireplace

I   hot plate

17 Which does **not** explain why the wind blows?

A   differences in the ability of Earth's land and water to absorb heat

B   the mixing of heat energy and light energy

C   the movement of heat energy from land and water to the surrounding air

D   the rising of warmer air

18 Which is evidence that Earth has changed over time?

F   fossils in sedimentary rocks

G   the number of animals on Earth

H   the size of Earth

I   the variety of animals on Earth

Name _____ Date _____

PLEASE NOTE

- **Use only a no. 2 pencil.**

- **Example:** ○●○○

- **Erase changes COMPLETELY.**

Earth and Space

Mark one answer for each question.

1 Ⓐ Ⓑ Ⓒ Ⓓ

2 Ⓕ Ⓖ Ⓗ Ⓘ

3 Ⓐ Ⓑ Ⓒ Ⓓ

4 Ⓕ Ⓖ Ⓗ Ⓘ

5 Ⓐ Ⓑ Ⓒ Ⓓ

6 Ⓕ Ⓖ Ⓗ Ⓘ

7 Ⓐ Ⓑ Ⓒ Ⓓ

8 Ⓕ Ⓖ Ⓗ Ⓘ

9 Ⓐ Ⓑ Ⓒ Ⓓ

10 Ⓕ Ⓖ Ⓗ Ⓘ

11 Ⓐ Ⓑ Ⓒ Ⓓ

12 Ⓕ Ⓖ Ⓗ Ⓘ

13 Ⓐ Ⓑ Ⓒ Ⓓ

14 Ⓕ Ⓖ Ⓗ Ⓘ

15 Ⓐ Ⓑ Ⓒ Ⓓ

16 Ⓕ Ⓖ Ⓗ Ⓘ

17 Ⓐ Ⓑ Ⓒ Ⓓ

18 Ⓕ Ⓖ Ⓗ Ⓘ

Physical Science

DIRECTIONS

Read each question carefully. Determine the best answer to the question from the answer choices provided. Then fill in the answer on your answer sheet.

1   Limestone and quartz are common minerals found in Florida. Sarah has a piece of each, but does not know which is which. To find out, she plans an investigation to determine the density of each sample, because limestone has a lower density than quartz. Density is equal to the mass divided by volume. She places a piece of each mineral into a graduated cylinder that contains water. The table shows the measurements Sarah recorded.

Mass of mineral 1 (g)	9.50
Mass of mineral 2 (g)	9
Volume of water in graduated cylinder (mL)	25
Volume of water and mineral 1 in graduated cylinder (mL)	30
Volume of water and mineral 2 in graduated cylinder (mL)	28.4

What can Sarah **most likely** conclude is true?

A   Mineral 2 is limestone because it has less mass.

B   Mineral 1 is limestone because it has more mass.

C   Mineral 1 is limestone because it has a lower density.

D   Mineral 2 is limestone because it has a lower density.

2   Jamie tests the physical and chemical properties of several elements in the laboratory. He finds that two of the elements have very similar properties. What can he conclude about these elements?

F   They have the same number of protons.

G   They have the same number of neutrons.

H   They are located in the same row of the periodic table.

I   They are located in the same column of the periodic table.

3   Troy investigates the density of an unknown piece of metal in the laboratory. Density is equal to mass divided by volume. The mass of the metal is 10.7 grams, and its volume is 1.5 cm^3. Based on the data in this table, what conclusion can Troy make about the unknown metal?

Metal	Density (g/cm^3)
gold	19.3
lead	11.4
silver	10.5
zinc	7.13

A   It is gold.

B   It is lead.

C   It is silver.

D   It is zinc.

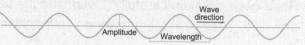

4 Diego and Samuel help to clean up a polluted stream. They collect a glass bottle filled with some juice, several wood sticks, and a plastic food container. How do the particles in the juice different from the particles in the glass, plastic, and wood?

F They are locked in place.

G They can move past one another.

H They move freely in all directions.

I They are locked in place, but can vibrate.

5 Which is **not** a sign of a chemical change?

A change in color

B change in shape

C formation of a gas

D formation of a solid

6 Which is **true** about how mass changes in physical and chemical changes?

F Mass is conserved in both physical and chemical changes.

G Mass is conserved in chemical changes, but not physical changes.

H Mass is not conserved in either physical or chemical changes.

I Mass is conserved in physical changes, but not chemical changes

7 Waves in the electromagnetic spectrum are classified by their frequencies. Which type of electromagnetic radiation has the highest frequency?

A gamma

B infrared

C radio

D x-ray

8 Light from the sun is an example of an electromagnetic wave such as the one shown. Based on the diagram, which is **true**?

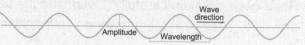

F All electromagnetic waves travel at the same speed.

G The amplitude measures the length of the wave.

H The wavelength is a measure of the energy of the wave.

I Wave period is the number of cycles per minute.

9 Maria is examining a straw in a glass of water. She observes that the straw appears bent when seen through the water from the side. What is the **best** explanation for this observation?

A Light is absorbed by the glass, causing the straw to appear bent.

B Light is reflected off the glass, causing the straw to appear bent.

C Light refracts when it enters the water, causing the straw to appear bent.

D Light is scattered when it enters the water, causing the straw to appear bent.

10 Sound waves travel at different speeds depending on the material they are traveling in. Which correctly orders how sound waves travel from slowest to fastest?

F   gas, liquid, solid

G   gas, solid, liquid

H   liquid, gas, solid

I   solid, liquid, gas

11 A carpenter hammers a nail into a piece of wood. Which choice **best** describes an energy transformation that is taking place?

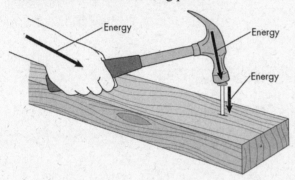

A   Kinetic energy is transformed into potential energy.

B   Mechanical energy is transformed into kinetic energy.

C   Potential energy is transformed into kinetic energy.

D   Potential energy is transformed into mechanical energy.

12 Which choice describes a transformation of kinetic energy into potential energy?

F   A boy rolls a bowling ball towards a set of pins.

G   A firefighter uses a water hose to put out a fire.

H   A girl places a heavy backpack on the floor.

I   A teacher places a book high on a shelf.

13 An astronaut finds his mass and weight on Earth. Which is **true** when the astronaut gets to the moon?

A   The astronaut's weight and mass will both decrease.

B   The astronaut's weight and mass will both increase.

C   The astronaut will weigh less, but his mass will increase.

D   The astronaut will weigh less, but his mass will remain the same.

14 Kit puts her metal spoon into a bowl of hot potatoes.

Which process takes place when the spoon comes in contact with the potatoes?

F   The average temperature of the spoon remains constant.

G   The potatoes transfer thermal energy to the spoon, causing the spoon to heat up.

H   The spoon transfers thermal energy to the potatoes, causing the potatoes to heat up.

I   The thermal energy of both the potatoes and the spoon increase.

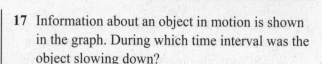

15 Mr. Tedesco has two metal cubes, one made of tin and the other made of silver. He heats the tin cube to 80°C and places the silver one in the freezer until it reaches 5°C. He places the cubes in a beaker containing water at 20°C. The cubes do not touch. Which **best** describes how heat will flow in the system?

A Heat flows from the silver cube into the tin cube.

B Heat flows from the silver cube into the water.

C Heat flows from the tin cube to the silver cube.

D Heat flows from the tin cube into the water.

16 Kelly is examining a sketch that shows the gravitational attraction between two objects.

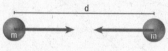

Which **best** describes the effect of distance on gravitational attraction between two objects?

F When the distance between two masses is decreased, the gravitational attraction decreases.

G When the distance between two masses is increased, the gravitational attraction remains constant.

H When the distance between two masses is increased, the gravitational attraction decreases.

I When the distance between two masses is increased, the gravitational attraction increases.

17 Information about an object in motion is shown in the graph. During which time interval was the object slowing down?

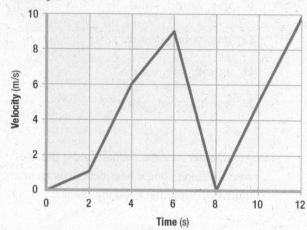

A 0–2 sec

B 2–6 sec

C 6–8 sec

D 8–12 sec

18 Which is **true** about unbalanced forces acting on an object?

F The force of friction decreases.

G The net force is 0 N.

H The object accelerates.

I The object does not move.

Name ______________________ Date __________

PLEASE NOTE
• Use only a no. 2 pencil.
• Example: ○●○○
• Erase changes COMPLETELY.

Physical Science

Mark one answer for each question.

1 Ⓐ Ⓑ Ⓒ Ⓓ
2 Ⓕ Ⓖ Ⓗ Ⓘ
3 Ⓐ Ⓑ Ⓒ Ⓓ
4 Ⓕ Ⓖ Ⓗ Ⓘ
5 Ⓐ Ⓑ Ⓒ Ⓓ
6 Ⓕ Ⓖ Ⓗ Ⓘ
7 Ⓐ Ⓑ Ⓒ Ⓓ
8 Ⓕ Ⓖ Ⓗ Ⓘ
9 Ⓐ Ⓑ Ⓒ Ⓓ
10 Ⓕ Ⓖ Ⓗ Ⓘ
11 Ⓐ Ⓑ Ⓒ Ⓓ
12 Ⓕ Ⓖ Ⓗ Ⓘ
13 Ⓐ Ⓑ Ⓒ Ⓓ
14 Ⓕ Ⓖ Ⓗ Ⓘ
15 Ⓐ Ⓑ Ⓒ Ⓓ
16 Ⓕ Ⓖ Ⓗ Ⓘ
17 Ⓐ Ⓑ Ⓒ Ⓓ
18 Ⓕ Ⓖ Ⓗ Ⓘ

Life Science

DIRECTIONS

Read each question carefully. Determine the best answer to the question from the answer choices provided. Then fill in the answer on your answer sheet.

1 Carbon is an element essential to all living things on Earth. Which **best** describes how carbon is transported in a food chain?

A Animals that eat plants consume carbon the plants took from the air.

B Carbon that is consumed by plants can never be consumed by an animal.

C Humans can consume carbon directly from the atmosphere.

D Plants consume sugars made of carbon found in the environment.

2 Karla is explaining cell theory to Jean. Which statement should Karla make?

F All cells are made of smaller cells.

G All cells are the same size.

H All cells come from existing cells.

I All cells have the same parts.

3 A fruit fly has the recessive trait of short wings. It is crossed with a fly, which is homozygous for the dominant allele of the gene and has the dominant trait of medium length wings.

What percentage of the offspring of this cross will **most likely** have the recessive trait of short wings?

A 0%

B 25%

C 50%

D 100%

4 A freshwater marsh is a type of ecosystem. Grasses, fish, wading birds, frogs, and alligators live together in freshwater marshes. Pieces of decaying material sink to the bottom of the marsh. In which places can carbon be found in the marsh?

F in living things and decaying materials only

G in living things only

H in the atmosphere and water only

I in the atmosphere, water, living things, and decaying materials

5 This diagram shows a single cell.

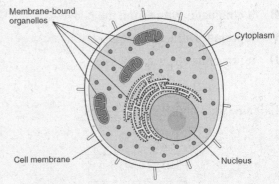

What is the function of the structure labeled Nucleus?

A to hold the cell's cell membrane

B to hold the cell's cytoplasm

C to hold the cell's DNA

D to hold the cell's organelles

6 Kevin is building a physical model of an animal cell. Which structure should Kevin **not** include in his model?

F cell membrane

G chloroplasts

H cytoplasm

I mitochondria

7 Look at the diagram of a human body system.

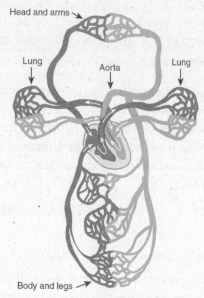

Head and arms →

Lung   Aorta   Lung

Body and legs →

Which **best** describes the role that this system plays in supporting the human body?

A It delivers oxygen and nutrients to cells.

B It eliminates waste from the body.

C It provides structural support.

D It transmits electrical messages.

8 Examine the Punnett square below.

	B	B
B	BB	BB
b	Bb	Bb

Which identifies the alleles of the parents shown here?

F *BB* and *BB*

G *BB* and *Bb*

H *Bb* and *Bb*

I *Bb* and *bb*

9 The Linnaean system of classification is used to group animals together based on how closely related scientists think organisms are. Which describes the **most closely** related organisms?

A Corals and jellyfish are in the same phylum.

B Lemurs and koala bears are in the same class.

C Seahorses and sea stars are in the same kingdom.

D Timberwolves and Bengal tigers are in the same order.

10 Gloria is comparing anatomical features of several organisms. She makes a diagram to show some similar characteristics that she observes.

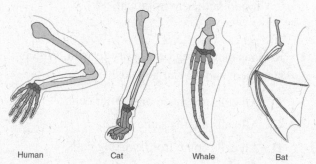

Human   Cat   Whale   Bat

Which **best** describes what Gloria's observations are evidence for?

F All of the organisms share a common ancestor.

G All of the organisms share a common lifestyle.

H All of the organisms share the same DNA.

I All of the organisms share the same habitat.

11 Kashi wanted to describe to his friend how living things are organized. Which **best** describes the pattern of organization in an organism?

A Cells are made of tissues.

B Organs can form organ systems.

C Some organs are made of cells.

D Tissues are more complex than organs.

12 A scientist studies different types of rats. The scientist finds a fossil that appears to be a rat skull, but it does not look exactly like any known rat species. What can the scientist **most likely** conclude about the organism?

   F The fossil specimen evolved over time into modern rats.

   G The fossil specimen is a species no longer alive today.

   H The fossil specimen is not related to any modern rats.

   I The fossil specimen lived in environments similar to those of modern rats.

13 A small population of lizards lives on an island where the environment is changing quickly. Which **best** describes why the lizards may become extinct?

   A The lizards are not able to reproduce.

   B The lizards are undergoing natural selection.

   C The lizards do not have enough genetic variation.

   D The lizards have too much overproduction.

14 Jasmine wants to describe how plant cells and animal cells are similar. Which statement should Jasmine **not** make about plant and animal cells?

   F Plant and animal cells both need carbon dioxide.

   G Plant and animal cells both produce energy.

   H Plant and animal cells both recycle waste products.

   I Plant and animal cells both require sugar.

15 Mangrove swamps are found along the southern coasts of Florida. A mangrove swamp contains an ecosystem of many organisms living among the large roots of the mangrove trees. This food web shows some of the relationships in that ecosystem.

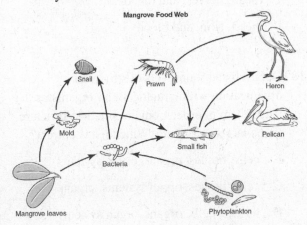

Mangrove Food Web

Which **best** describes how the organisms act in the food web?

   A Herons and pelicans prey upon one another.

   B Mangroves are the only producers shown.

   C Phytoplankton act as consumers of bacteria.

   D Small fish and prawns compete for bacteria.

16 Remoras are small fish that attach to sharks but do not harm them. When sharks tear prey apart, remoras eat the leftovers. What relationship do remoras have with sharks?

   F commensalism

   G mutualism

   H parasitism

   I predator-prey

17 What are the main structures of the cardiovascular system?

   A heart, blood, and blood vessels

   B heart, lungs, and blood

   C heart, nerves, and blood

   D heart, skin, and blood

18 Gerard listed four levels of structural organization within multicellular organisms. He listed them in order from the smallest structure to the largest structure. Which list is correct?

   F cells, tissues, organs, organ systems

   G cells, tissues, organ systems, organs

   H tissues, cells, organs, organ systems

   I tissues, cells, organ systems, organs

Life Science

PLEASE NOTE
• Use only a no. 2 pencil.
• Example: ◯●◯◯
• Erase changes COMPLETELY.

Life Science
Mark one answer for each question.

1 Ⓐ Ⓑ Ⓒ Ⓓ

2 Ⓕ Ⓖ Ⓗ Ⓘ

3 Ⓐ Ⓑ Ⓒ Ⓓ

4 Ⓕ Ⓖ Ⓗ Ⓘ

5 Ⓐ Ⓑ Ⓒ Ⓓ

6 Ⓕ Ⓖ Ⓗ Ⓘ

7 Ⓐ Ⓑ Ⓒ Ⓓ

8 Ⓕ Ⓖ Ⓗ Ⓘ

9 Ⓐ Ⓑ Ⓒ Ⓓ

10 Ⓕ Ⓖ Ⓗ Ⓘ

11 Ⓐ Ⓑ Ⓒ Ⓓ

12 Ⓕ Ⓖ Ⓗ Ⓘ

13 Ⓐ Ⓑ Ⓒ Ⓓ

14 Ⓕ Ⓖ Ⓗ Ⓘ

15 Ⓐ Ⓑ Ⓒ Ⓓ

16 Ⓕ Ⓖ Ⓗ Ⓘ

17 Ⓐ Ⓑ Ⓒ Ⓓ

18 Ⓕ Ⓖ Ⓗ Ⓘ

SC.8.N.1.1 Define a problem from the eighth grade curriculum using appropriate reference materials to support scientific understanding, plan and carry out scientific investigation of various types, such as systematic observations or experiments, identify variables, collect and organize data, interpret data in charts, tables, and graphics, analyze information, make predictions, and defend conclusions.

Scientific Investigations

Defining a Problem

Before you begin a scientific investigation, you must identify what you will study. In other words, you must define a problem. In science, a problem does not have to be a negative issue, such as the word is used in everyday language. A scientific problem is a specific question that a scientist wants to answer. The problem must be well-defined, or precisely stated so that it can be investigated.

For example, you might ask, "What factors cause seedlings to grow best?" This question is too vague because it can depend on a number of different factors, and because determining what is best depends on opinion. Instead, you need to limit and define what you want to know. Here are several well-defined questions that you might ask:

- How does the amount of available light affect seedling height?
- How does the amount of water in the soil affect seedling height?
- How does acid rain affect the color of seedlings?

Forming a Hypothesis and Making Predictions

Scientists develop a hypothesis based on a question. A **hypothesis** is a possible answer to the question. Unlike a wild guess, a hypothesis is based on research along with prior knowledge and observations. Scientists test the hypothesis to see if it is true. Before testing a hypothesis, scientists make predictions about what will happen in an investigation.

One way to test a hypothesis is to conduct an **experiment**, which is an organized procedure to study something under controlled conditions. In an experiment, scientists change or control certain factors, such as temperature, amount of light, or

presence of a chemical. Only one variable at a time is changed. An **independent variable** is the factor that is deliberately changed during an investigation. A **dependent variable** changes as a result of manipulation of the independent variable. A controlled experiment should have just one independent variable. Scientists try to keep other variables constant, or unchanged, so they do not affect the results. In this way, they know that any changes observed resulted from changes in the independent variable. For example, suppose a scientist changes the amount of light a plant receives, and then measures the height of the plant over time. The scientist changed the amount of light, so it is the independent variable. The height of the plant depended on the amount of light, so height is the dependent variable.

The hypothesis is usually presented in the form of a statement that relates the variables. For example, a hypothesis might be "If the amount of light a plant receives increases, then the plant will grow taller." In this hypothesis statement, the independent variable is the amount of light, and the dependent variable is the height of the plant.

Collecting and Organizing Data

In a comparative investigation, you collect and compare data. For example, you might grow seedlings under different conditions, such as darkness, dim light, and bright light, and use a control sample of seedlings. Tables and graphs are methods of summarizing data in a way that is easy to analyze and look for patterns. A table uses columns and rows to list data in an organized way. The graph below lists the number of minutes to double a bacterial population at different temperatures.

Temperature (°C)	Minutes to double bacterial population
10	130
20	60
30	29
40	19
50	No growth

Data can also be represented visually in graphs. There are different types of graphs depending on the data. For example, change that occurs over time might be represented on a line graph, whereas parts of a whole might be represented on a circle graph. The graph below relates hair length to time. Without identifying all of the points on the graph, you can easily see that length increases over time by the upward slant of the line.

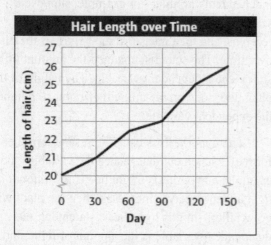

Keep in mind that not all investigations can be controlled. Some investigations must be descriptive. In a descriptive investigation, you collect data and record observations. For example, you could observe and record how something looks, smells, sounds, or feels. (Do not taste anything in the lab unless your teacher instructs it.) This method of conducting investigations is very useful when directly observing events in nature, such as when biologists observe animal behavior.

Drawing and Defending Conclusions

Scientists conclude whether the results of their investigation support the hypothesis. If not, scientists may think more about the problem and come up with a new problem to test. Or they may repeat the experiment to see if any mistakes were made. When the scientists publish their results, they must be prepared to defend their conclusions if they are challenged by other scientists. Hypotheses are valuable if they lead to research and discoveries that help us find out more about the natural word. This is true even if those hypotheses are not supported by the results of an experiment.

Scientific Method

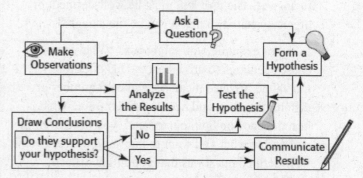

The process of answering a scientific question is often described by a series of events known as the scientific method. Keep in mind that there is no single method for answering a question, nor is there one correct order of events. Instead, there is a general procedure that is represented in the flow chart. For example, the diagram shows that after you ask a question, you might form a hypothesis. At that point, you might make more observations, or you might test the hypothesis. Once you gather and analyze the results, you can draw a conclusion about whether or not the hypothesis was supported. If it is supported, after repeated investigations, you might communicate your results. If it is not supported, you might form a new hypothesis and begin again.

Student-Response Activity

1 A student plans to investigate the motion of a toy car on ramps at different heights. She plans to change the height of the ramp by stacking different amounts of books under it. The table shows how the student plans to collect data in the experiment.

Number of books	Height of ramp	Distance traveled
1		
2		

What are the variables in this investigation?

independent variable _____

dependent variable _____

2 A scientist proposed a hypothesis that burning coal at higher altitudes would release less pollution. The data the scientist collected did not support the hypothesis. In what way is the hypothesis still valuable?

_____

_____

_____

3 Write a hypothesis that relates the independent variable of temperature to the dependent variable of number of flowers on a plant.

If _____ , then _____ .

Read the scenario and look at the data in the table. Then answer Questions 4 and 5.

A scientist measured the downward speed of a falling object at 1-second intervals. The results are summarized in the data table.

Time (s)	Speed (m/s)
0	0
1	9.8
2	19.6
3	29.4
4	39.2

4 Based on the data, what can you predict about the downward speed at the end of 5 seconds? Explain.

_____

_____

_____

5 Why is it useful to organize the data on a graph? Explain your answer.

_____

_____

_____

Benchmark Assessment SC.8.N.1.1

Fill in the letter of the best choice.

1 Which is a scientific question that can be tested?

Ⓐ What is electricity?

Ⓑ Which is the nicest color for rose plants?

Ⓒ How many pine trees are in a tundra forest?

Ⓓ Does water heat up more quickly than sand in sunlight?

2 A scientist is raising the temperature of a sample of water to find out if the amount of salt that can be mixed into the water changes. Which is the independent variable in this investigation?

Ⓕ the amount of water in the sample

Ⓖ the temperature of the water

Ⓗ the amount of salt that mixes in the water

Ⓘ the type of salt mixed into the water

3 Which must be **true** of any hypothesis for it to be useful in a scientific investigation?

Ⓐ It must be supported by data.

Ⓑ It must be used to develop a theory.

Ⓒ It must lead to further investigations.

Ⓓ It must be developed without depending on prior investigations.

4 The diagram shows steps a scientist might follow when conducting an investigation.

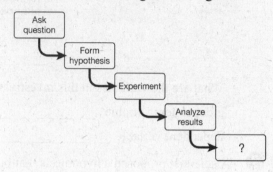

Which should replace the question mark in the final step?

Ⓕ develop a theory

Ⓖ draw a conclusion

Ⓗ select equipment

Ⓘ identify the variables

5 Which **best** describes an experiment?

Ⓐ A scientist measures the height of crops that received different fertilizers.

Ⓑ A scientist measures the speed at which an eagle travels while it is hunting.

Ⓒ A scientist measures the diameter of a certain type of tree throughout a forest.

Ⓓ A scientist measures the rate at which a population of wild insects reproduces.

SC.7.N.1.2 Differentiate replication (by others) from repetition (multiple trials).

Repetition and Replication

Supporting a Scientific Investigation

Once a scientist performs an investigation, he or she draws a conclusion about whether or not the results supported the hypothesis. If the hypothesis is supported, what should the scientist do next? The temptation may be to announce the results to the scientific community, but it would be much too soon. The results of a single investigation do not supply enough evidence to validate the hypothesis.

Repetition

The first step to confirming the results of an investigation is to repeat the study. Multiple repetitions of an investigation that produce similar results provide support for the findings. For example, suppose you follow a recipe to bake chocolate chip cookies. The first batch is delicious so you decide to bake another batch. Unfortunately, the next batch does not taste as good. You were not able to repeat the results from the first batch. It might be that you did not follow the recipe exactly as you had the first time, or maybe the temperature of your oven was not the same as it was the first time. Whatever the reason, you cannot confirm that the recipe is a good one until it can be used to produce the same delicious cookies at least three times.

A similar process occurs in science. Suppose a scientist places a piece of *Elodea* in a beaker of water, placing it some distance away from a light source. The scientist counts the number of bubbles released from the plant every minute for five minutes total. The results are in the table.

Bubbles Released from the *Elodea* Plant

Time (min)	Number of bubbles when light is 10 cm away	Number of bubbles when light is 20 cm away
1	25	9
2	26	10
3	28	8
4	25	10
5	21	9

The scientist analyzes the results and draws a conclusion that the number of bubbles produced decreases with distance. Before the scientist should consider the conclusion valid, he or she must conduct the same experiment several more times. If multiple experiments produce similar results, the scientist can consider the results to be reliable.

Replication

Another way to confirm the results of an investigation is for another scientist to replicate the experiment. Before results can be considered valid, many different scientists must be able to repeat the investigation and replicate the results. Reproduction of the findings by different scientists in different locations to ensure accuracy is known as *replication*.

Think again about the cookie example. Suppose you made the recipe three times, and the results were the same each time. You give the cookie recipe to a friend. Unfortunately, your friend's cookies do not taste as good as yours. Your friend was not able to replicate the results. It might be that your friend did not follow the recipe exactly as you had, or maybe your friend's oven was slightly hotter than yours. Whatever the reason, you cannot confirm that the recipe is a good one until someone else uses it to produce the same delicious cookies.

Think again about the Elodea investigation described earlier. If another scientist tries to replicate the investigation, he or she needs to repeat the procedure in the same exact way as in the original experiment. The scientist will need to use the same size and type of beaker, the same amount of water, and the same length of Elodea. If the scientist does everything in the same way and gets the same results, it can help validate the results. It would take many replications to reach such a conclusion, but this is a good start.

If the scientist repeats the Elodea investigation but gets different results, he or she will need to find out why. It could be because the previous scientist made an error or changed some aspect of the investigation. Or it could be because the original conclusion was not valid. That is why it is important for scientists to repeat investigations.

Student-Response Activity

For Questions 1–5, read the descriptions and identify each one as *replication* or *repetition*.

1 Thomas measured the masses of 4 different objects. His lab partner then made the same measurements to see if he gets the same results.

_____

2 A scientist measures the temperature of a local lake each day at noon for one month.

_____

3 Francis asks Lillian, a chemist, for her procedure so he can confirm Lillian's results.

_____

4 Kelsee reviewed the work of a biologist in a scientific journal. Kelsee plans to do the same experiments to find out if she gets the same results.

_____

5 Mariah places six identical pails of water in sunlight and measures the temperature of the water in each pail every 10 minutes.

_____

6 Explain the difference between repetition and replication.

_____

_____

_____

_____

_____

7 A scientist stirred a substance into 100 g of water at three different temperatures until it stopped dissolving into the water. Examine the table of the scientist's recorded results.

	Trial 1 mass of substance (g)	Trial 2 mass of substance (g)	Trial 3 mass of substance (g)
Room Temperature	110	72	105
Cold	81	55	78
Hot	135	83	140

During which trial did the scientist most likely commit an error in the procedure? How do you know?

_____

_____

_____

_____

_____

8 Why is it important for the results of an investigation to be replicable?

_____

_____

_____

_____

_____

_____

Benchmark Assessment SC.7.N.1.2

Fill in the letter of the best choice.

1 A scientist announces that he has found a new way to produce energy. Why is it important for other scientists to replicate the results?

(A) to include more scientists in the development of the new energy source

(B) to confirm that the results are valid and not the result of errors

(C) to make sure that all scientists know how to perform the same investigation

(D) to find ways to make the investigation easier to perform

2 Brian conducts an investigation. He follows the procedure below:

Step 1: Hold a golf ball at a height of 50 cm, and let go.

Step 2: With a partner, measure the height to which the ball bounces.

Step 3: Drop the ball 10 more times from the same height.

Step 4: Find the average height to which the ball bounces.

Which step indicates repetition?

(F) Step 1

(G) Step 2

(H) Step 3

(I) Step 4

3 Zachery conducts an investigation involving cells. He finds that adding a certain chemical to a cell causes it to make a protein that humans need to stay healthy. What should Zachery do next?

(A) repeat the investigation to see if he gets the same results

(B) publish the results in a scientific journal

(C) hold a press conference to announce the discovery

(D) destroy the procedure so that no one else can repeat it

4 Leah heats a sample of an unknown solid until it melts into a liquid. Which describes an example of replication related to Leah's investigation?

(F) Tina continues to heat the sample until it turns into a gas.

(G) Juan lets the sample cool and then heats it again.

(H) Victor heats a different sample with the same mass until it melts.

(I) Raquel heats an identical sample to see if it melts at the same temperature.

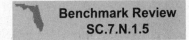
SC.7.N.1.5 Describe the methods used in the pursuit of a scientific explanation as seen in different fields of science such as biology, geology, and physics.

Methods and Models Used in Different Fields of Science

When investigating a scientific question, it is important to use appropriate methods and tools. For example, you would not use a microscope to study a distant star. Similarly, you would not use a measuring cup to estimate the amount of water in a lake. The method you use to gather scientific information can also vary across different fields of science.

Scientific Technology

In choosing a scientific method to follow, scientists may also choose technology that helps with an investigation. Technology is the use of scientific knowledge and processes to solve practical problems. Scientists use technology to store and display data, perform calculations on data, and communicate information. Scientists also use different types of technology to obtain information from remote locations, collect samples, and make measurements. Use of a hand lens to examine the features of a tree leaf is a simple form of technology. Use of a satellite that relays images about weather conditions to Earth is a more complex form of technology.

Scientific Models

Scientists use information they have gathered to make models. A scientific **model** is a visual or mathematical representation of an object or a system. Models are used in science to help explain how something works or to describe how something is structured. Models can also be used to make predictions or explain observations. Some examples of scientific models include physical models, mathematical models, and conceptual models.

To be truly useful, a model must be in proportion with the object it represents. So, a model must have a scale that relates to the object, much like a map has a scale that relates to actual distances.

For example, suppose a model represents a river that is 100 km long. If 1 cm on the model represents 10 km, the model must be 10 cm long.

A model must be accurate. Otherwise, it will be misleading. Even when models are accurate, they have limitations because it is never exactly like the real thing it represents. For example, a model of a body may show the parts of the body, but does not act like a human body would. Even so, the model is useful for understanding how the parts of the body are related.

Physical Models A physical model is one that you can touch and see. A toy rocket and a plastic skeleton are examples of physical models. Drawings and diagrams are also physical models. Many physical models look like the thing they represent, but may not represent every aspect of it.

Mathematical Models A mathematical model may be made up of numbers, equations, and other forms of data. Some of these models are fairly simple and can be used easily. For example, a Punnett square is a model of how traits are passed from parents to offspring. By relating traits in a square diagram, scientists can predict how often certain traits will appear in the offspring of two parents. Other mathematical models are quite complex, and often require computers to make and manipulate them.

Conceptual Models A conceptual model is a description of an idea. For example, the idea that life originated from chemicals is a conceptual model. This type of model develops an idea based on reasoning and evidence and may include the other types of models to express information.

Investigating Geology

Models that scientists develop can vary based on the field of science. For example, geologists study Earth's physical structure and composition. Geologists often study Earth by taking samples of rocks, soil, or other materials; however, some features on Earth are difficult or impossible to study closeup. For example, active volcanoes are both large and dangerous. So scientists use technology to gather data from a distance. They also make models of different types of volcanoes that show how the parts of the volcanoes interact.

Geologists also use models to represent objects or processes that they cannot see. For example, Earth's layers and core are too deep to view directly. Scientists use different types of technology, such as seismographs used to study earthquake waves, to gather information about Earth's interior. They use this information to make models that represent the composite and thickness of Earth's layers.

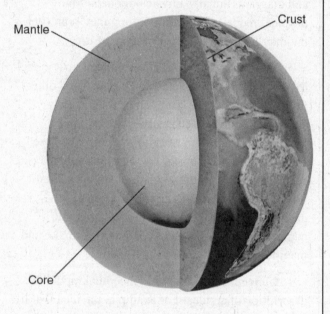

Mantle

Crust

Core

Investigating Biology

Biology is the study of living things. Some parts of the natural world are too small to observe with the unaided eye. Many organisms, such as bacteria, fall into this category. Parts of organisms, such as plant and animal cells, are also too small to observe without technology. Scientists use different types of technology, such as powerful microscopes, to gather information about these small objects. They then use this information to develop models that enlarge the objects to represent their parts and interactions.

Other models in biology represent processes and systems. A model of the circulatory system, for example, can show differences among smaller parts such as arteries, veins, and capillaries. It can also allow you to trace the flow of blood from one part of the body to another.

Investigating Physics

Physics is the study of matter and motion, as well as force and energy. All matter in the universe is made up of particles that are too small to see even with powerful light microscopes. These particles include atoms and molecules and the subatomic particles within them. Scientists gather information about atoms using different types of technology, including electron microscopes. Scientists also use incredibly large, powerful machines called particle accelerators to gather data about subatomic particles. Scientists use this information to develop models that show what they know about particles and their interactions.

While specific tools and methods differ depending upon the scientific field of study, the systematic, evidence-based approach to gathering data remains the same.

Student-Response Activity

❶ Match each type of model to its description.

_____ physical model

_____ mathematical model

_____ conceptual model

A. Model that explains a system by describing an idea or thought, and may use other types of models to do so

B. Model that represents a system by making a copy of it on a larger or smaller scale

C. Model that describes a system using numbers, equations, or related terms

❷ Scientists often use computers to record data and perform calculations on them. How does the use of a computer help a scientist?

_____

_____

❸ Why would a model of Earth's layers be helpful when studying Earth's interior?

_____

_____

❹ Gregor uses clay to make a physical model of a volcano. Describe one advantage of the model and one limitation.

_____

_____

_____

_____

❺ Compare and contrast reasons why scientists use models in biology and physics.

_____

_____

_____

❻ Many scientific models change over time. Why does this happen, and what does it indicate about science?

_____

_____

_____

Benchmark Assessment SC.7.N.1.5

Fill in the letter of the best choice.

❶ A student makes a physical model of an atom using toothpicks and foam balls.

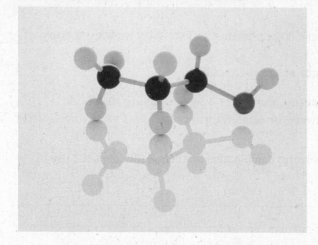

What is a limitation of this physical model of an atom?

Ⓐ It cannot show the components that make up an atom.

Ⓑ It is not based on experimental data collected by scientists.

Ⓒ It cannot show the interactions that exist between the parts.

Ⓓ It does not show the general structure of an atom.

❷ The process of photosynthesis, which takes place in green plants, is represented by the model below.

$6CO_2 + 6H_2O \rightarrow C_6H_{12}O_6 + 6O_2$

What type of model is shown?

Ⓕ computer model

Ⓖ conceptual model

Ⓘ physical model

Ⓗ mathematical model

❸ Upon completing an investigation, Mellissa summarizes the work in a lab report. Which title **most likely** indicates that the student used a model to prepare the report?

Ⓐ The Proper Use of Lab Equipment

Ⓑ Safety Procedures to Follow at All Times

Ⓒ Using the International System of Units (SI)

Ⓓ Comparing the Sizes of Planets in the Solar System

❹ A telescope is a type of technology used to study the moons of other planets. How does this technology help scientists?

Ⓕ It brings the objects closer to Earth.

Ⓖ It enables scientists to visit the moons.

Ⓗ It makes the moons appear closer than they are.

Ⓘ It makes the moons larger than they are.

SC.6.N.2.2 Explain that scientific knowledge is durable because it is open to change as new evidence or interpretations are encountered.

How Science Progresses

Scientific Ideas

Scientific knowledge gives us the most reliable methods of understanding nature. Scientific knowledge and discoveries are long-lasting and reliable due to the ways in which they are developed. It takes time for new ideas to develop into scientific theories or to become accepted as scientific laws. Scientific knowledge that scientists question today was formed over hundreds, or even thousands, of years.

An idea is only considered a scientific one if it can be tested and supported by evidence. The process of building scientific knowledge never ends as it can change over time as discoveries and new data continue to raise questions. As a result, scientists explore these questions. If their answers do not support the original idea, then the idea must change. Scientists should always use scientific methods to test new ideas.

New Evidence Changes Scientific Knowledge

The study of astronomy illustrates how scientific knowledge can change over time. Almost everything that the earliest astronomers knew about the universe came from what they could discover with their eyes and minds. The Greek philosopher, Ptolemy, thought that Earth was at the center of the universe and that the other planets and the sun revolved around Earth. Then, in 1543, Copernicus published a theory that the sun was at the center of the universe and that all of the planets—including Earth—orbit the sun. His theory was based on observations he made of the movement of the planets. In 1609, Johannes Kepler proposed that all of the planets revolve around the sun in elliptical orbits, and that the sun is not in the exact center of the orbits. He used data he collected about the positions of the planets at different times as evidence to support his argument. In 1687, Isaac Newton stated that all objects in the universe attract each other through gravitational force and explained why

all of the planets orbit the most massive object in the solar system—the sun. Based on the work of Kepler and others, Newton developed a very accurate model of the solar system.

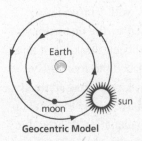

Geocentric Model

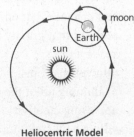

Heliocentric Model

Evidence Helps Ideas Grow

Isaac Newton made many contributions to multiple fields of mathematics and science. His ideas about gravity, for example, helped to shape scientific knowledge for hundreds of years. Newton's law of gravity states that all matter in the universe exerts an attractive force on all the other matter in the universe. It also states that the strength of that force depends on the masses of the objects, which are attracting each other, and on the distance between them.

In 1798, more than one hundred years after Newton first described the law of gravity, a scientist named Henry Cavendish accurately measured the gravitational constant. Newton's ideas and the evidence gathered by Cavendish enabled people to accurately predict the motion of objects in our solar system. Newton's ideas were tested over and over again.

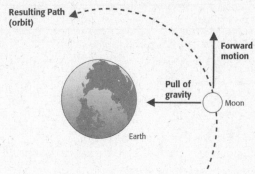

All of the observations scientists made and data they gathered from experiments were considered empirical evidence. Because all the evidence supported Newton's ideas, they were unchanged for hundreds of years.

Creative Thinking Leads to New Discoveries

Newton's law of gravity remained unchanged until the twentieth century. In 1915, Albert Einstein published his theory of general relativity. Einstein showed that gravitation depended not only on mass and distance, but on time as well. Einstein also realized that gravity is caused by the distortion of space and time. Newton had been thinking in three dimensions; Einstein introduced the fourth. By examining all of the evidence, reasoning logically, and using creativity, Einstein was able to come up with a new and improved explanation of how the universe works. While Newton's ideas about gravitation are still used today to perform basic calculations, Einstein's ideas have allowed scientists to make much more precise and accurate calculations when studying extremely massive objects.

When Einstein first introduced his theory, it was not immediately accepted. Scientists all around the world discussed and scrutinized Einstein's work, with many people doubting that he was correct. Then, in 1919, an opportunity to test Einstein's theory presented itself. One feature of Einstein's theory was that massive objects, such as the sun, actually cause space to curve around them. If this were true, then light from a distant star would be able to travel around the sun. When a solar eclipse occurred that year, scientists observed a star that should have been behind the disk of the sun. This meant that the light from the star did not simply travel in a straight line and run into the sun. Instead, it followed a curved path, and was visible to observers on Earth. This new piece of evidence supported Einstein's theory. General relativity was one of the most important discoveries in the entire history of science. Nonetheless, new evidence may someday lead to general relativity being revised or replaced.

Student-Response Activity

1 Write out the steps of how a scientific idea can be revised. Include at least three steps.

_____

_____

_____

_____

_____

_____

_____

2 Long ago, people thought that the sun revolved around Earth. Explain why our model of how the solar system works has changed since the year 1500. Include at least two reasons, as evidence, why it changed.

_____

_____

_____

_____

_____

_____

_____

_____

3 Match the phrases on the left with the correct term on the right.

_____   looking through a telescope at a star   **A.** evidence

_____   data gathered by scientifically testing ideas   **B.** experiment

_____   thinking a problem through to find an answer   **C.** observation

_____   testing what happens under controlled conditions   **D.** reasoning

4 Identify an example of a scientific idea from the past that has been changed. Describe what evidence caused the idea to change.

_____

_____

_____

_____

_____

_____

Benchmark Assessment SC.6.N.2.2

Fill in the letter of the best choice.

1 Scientific knowledge can be changed. Which would **most likely** lead to a change?

(A) A scientist makes observations to test an older idea.

(B) A scientist raises new questions about an older idea.

(C) A scientist has a new idea that goes against an older idea.

(D) A scientist collects data that fails to support an older idea.

2 Which choice describes the collection of evidence?

(F) Scientists examine ideas and debate them.

(G) Scientists make many observations of a single object.

(H) Scientists write out their findings in scientific journals.

(I) Scientists decide what the results of an experiment mean.

3 Which is the **most important** factor in deciding whether an idea is scientifically valid?

(A) simplicity or complexity of the idea

(B) data from observations or experiments

(C) debate and consensus among scientists

(D) the length of time that an idea has been around

4 The heliocentric model of the solar system states that all objects in the solar system orbit the sun. Which statement explains why scientists accept this model?

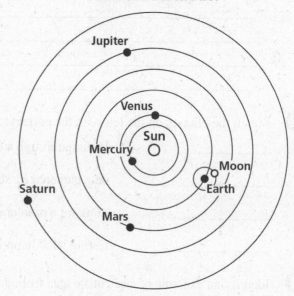

Heliocentric model

(F) It is an exact description of how the solar system actually works.

(G) It is a close approximation of how the solar system actually works.

(H) It is an idea that was developed over time based on many observations.

(I) It is a better model than the geocentric model because it is much simpler.

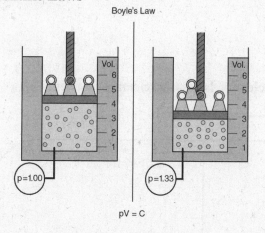
SC.7.N.3.1 Recognize and explain the difference between theories and laws and give several examples of scientific theories and the evidence that supports them.

Scientific Laws and Theories

What Science Tells Us

You may think that what you find out in science is accepted by everyone and unchanging. That is not always true. The "facts" of science are simply the most widely accepted explanations. Scientific knowledge is and probably always will be changing. To understand the nature of scientific knowledge, you must understand how scientists use certain words. *Law* and *theory* are two familiar words that have very specific scientific meanings.

Scientific Laws

Boyle's Law

$pV = C$

A scientific **law** is a description of a specific relationship under given conditions in the natural world. Scientific laws describe how the world works. They are scientific principles that work without exception to predict or explain nature under specific conditions.

Laws are typically statements, which can be written as mathematical equations. The law of conservation of energy states that energy in a system can neither be created nor destroyed. This is fairly easy to understand conceptually. Another

example of a law is Boyle's law, which states that the pressure and volume of a gas are inversely proportional. Boyle's law can be written as $pV = C$, meaning that the pressure of a gas multiplied by its volume will always give the same value (the constant C).

Even though *law* may sound better established or more concrete than *theory*, laws are still subject to change. Newton's law of gravitation, for example, was considered to be complete until Einstein introduced his theory of relativity.

Scientific Theory of Evolution

The scientific theory of evolution is an example of a theory. Evolution is the process in which inherited characteristics within a population change over generations, sometimes giving rise to new species. Scientists continue to develop theories to explain how evolution happens. When Charles Darwin first wrote about evolution by natural selection, he did not know about the laws of inheritance or the molecular basis of traits. As scientists have learned more about these two fields of study, they have improved upon Darwin's explanation for how species change over time.

Much of the strongest evidence supporting the scientific theory of evolution comes from the fossil record. As paleontologists have uncovered more fossils, a more complete set of data has become available to scientists to revise the theory of evolution. Today, scientists understand that there are many intricacies in how species evolve, and not all scientists agree on exactly how evolution occurs. Nearly all scientists agree, though, that the theory of evolution accurately explains how new species have appeared on Earth over time.

Another scientific theory is the theory of plate tectonics. When we look at our planet, we can generally see only the surface. Many features of Earth's surface are visible, such as mountains, volcanoes, and deep ocean basins. For most of human history, people came up with stories to explain how these landforms came to be. Scientists began to investigate questions that people had and to collect evidence to support their answers. Scientists discovered that large sections of Earth's surface move as units, called plates. Parts of plates collide with other plates, forming mountains and volcanoes. For example, along the Pacific coast of the United States, there are many tall mountains and even some volcanoes. These landforms are the result of the North American Plate and the Pacific Plate colliding.

Even though we cannot observe the plates themselves directly, the **theory of plate tectonics** allows us to explain many features that we can observe.

Theory of Plate Tectonics

Tectonic Plates

Student-Response Activity

❶ Complete the Venn diagram to compare and contrast scientific laws with scientific theories.

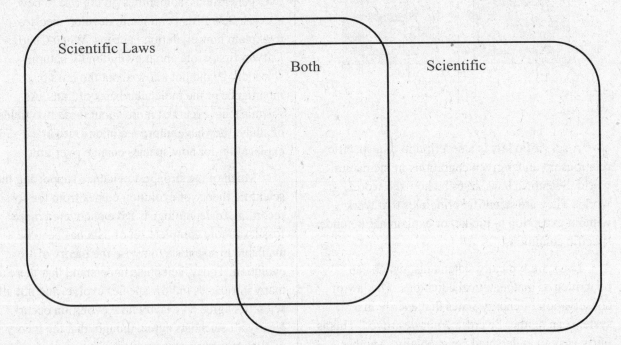

Scientific Laws   Both   Scientific

❷ Your friend claims to have developed a new theory. How could you decide if your friend's theory is a scientific theory?

_____

_____

_____

_____

_____

_____

❸ Read the statements and identify each as a *scientific law* or a *scientific theory*.

A scientist explains that the planets always move in an ellipse around the sun.

_____

A scientist explains that the energy of a photon is proportional to the wavelength of light, or E=hf.

_____

Scientists agree that planets form in a disk around a new star. This explains why the planets are all on the same orbital plane.

_____

Scientists agree that the offspring of any cross between two parent organisms receives 50% of its DNA from each parent.

_____

A scientist explains that not all organisms survive equally well, and the traits that help animals survive are most likely to be passed on.

_____

Benchmark Assessment SC.7.N.3.1

Fill in the letter of the best choice.

1 Which is a **true** statement about the scientific theory of evolution?

(A) It was accepted by all scientists without question.

(B) It proved what most scientists believed at that time.

(C) It had no significant impact on scientific thought and society.

(D) It was developed using large amounts of empirical evidence.

2 Which is a **true** statement about scientific laws?

(F) Scientific laws are the same thing as facts.

(G) Scientific laws can explain a wide range of events.

(H) Scientific laws can change in light of new evidence.

(I) Scientific laws are the foundations of scientific theories.

3 Which **best** explains why scientists accept the theory of relativity as a valid scientific theory?

(A) Scientists have found an example of how the theory of relativity is true.

(B) Scientists recognize that Albert Einstein was the smartest scientist ever.

(C) Scientists believe what is agreed upon by the majority of other scientists.

(D) Scientists are able to explain many natural events by applying the theory.

4 An engineer claims to know the exact amount of energy it takes to move roller coaster cars to the top of a track. The engineer uses the same formula to calculate the energy needed to move any object. Which **best** describes how the engineer can know the right amount of energy?

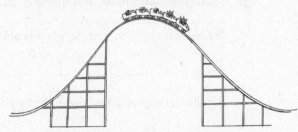

(F) The engineer uses a theory, because the engineer can explain the motion of any object.

(G) The engineer uses a law, because it is a formula that can be applied without exception.

(H) The engineer uses a theory, because the calculations are based on evidence.

(I) The engineer uses a law, because the motion of objects is a real world problem, not a theoretical one.

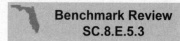

SC.8.E.5.3 Distinguish the hierarchal relationships between planets and other astronomical bodies relative to solar system, galaxy, and universe, including distance, size, and composition.

Our Place in the Universe

The Solar System

The solar system is divided into two main parts—the inner solar system and the outer solar system. The inner solar system contains the four planets closest to the sun. The outer solar system contains the planets farthest from the sun.

The inner planets, also called terrestrial planets, are very dense and rocky. These planets are smaller, denser, and rockier than the outer planets. Mercury is the smallest planet and is closest to the sun. Mercury has very little atmosphere. Venus is more like Earth than any other planet. Venus is only slightly smaller, less massive, and less dense than Earth. Of the terrestrial planets, Venus has the densest atmosphere; it has 90 times the pressure of Earth's atmosphere! The air on Venus is mostly carbon dioxide, but it is also made of some of the most destructive acids known. Mars is half the diameter of Earth. Because of its thinner atmosphere and greater distance from the sun, Mars is a cold planet.

The outer planets—Jupiter, Saturn, Uranus, and Neptune—are very large and are composed mostly of gases. As a result, these planets are known as gas giants. Since the gas giants are much more massive than the inner planets, they have much greater diameters. The outer planets are composed primarily of hydrogen and helium. Their atmospheres blend smoothly into the denser layers of their interiors. Until 2006, Pluto was considered the ninth planet. Astronomers have since classified it, along with other small icy bodies far from the sun, as a minor planet.

Orbiting most of the planets are smaller bodies called moons. Earth has only one moon, but Jupiter has more than 60. The rest of our solar system is made up of other small bodies. These include dwarf planets, comets, asteroids, and meteoroids. Altogether, there are up to a trillion small bodies in the solar system.

The Solar System

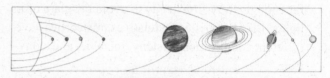

Other Astronomical Bodies

The solar system contains not only planets and moons, but also other small bodies, including comets, asteroids, and meteoroids. Scientists study these objects to find out more about the composition of our solar system. A small body of ice, rock, and cosmic dust loosely packed together is called a **comet**. Some scientists refer to comets as "dirty snowballs" because of their composition. Comets form in the cold, outer solar system. When a comet passes close enough to the sun, solar radiation warms the ice so that the comet gives off gas and dust in the form of a long tail. A comet can have two different tails at the same time—an ion tail of charged particles and a dust tail of uncharged particles. The solid center of a comet is called its **nucleus**. Comet nuclei can range in size from less than half a kilometer to more than 100 km in diameter. Comets orbit in long, stretched out ellipses.

Small, rocky bodies that revolve around the sun are called **asteroids**. They range from a few meters to more than 900 km in diameter. Asteroids have irregular shapes, although some larger ones are spherical. Most asteroids orbit the sun in the **asteroid belt**, a wide region between the orbits of Mars and Jupiter. Like comets, asteroids are thought to be material left over from the formation of the solar system.

A **meteoroid** is a small, rocky body that revolves around the sun. It is similar to, but much smaller than, an asteroid. In fact, most meteoroids are probably pieces of asteroids. A meteoroid that enters Earth's atmosphere and strikes the ground is called a **meteorite**.

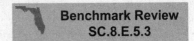
From the ground, you see a spectacular streak of light, or a shooting star. A **meteor** is the bright streak of light caused by a meteoroid or comet dust burning up in the atmosphere.

Many meteors we see come from very small (dust-sized to pebble-sized) rocks. Even so, meteors can be seen on almost any night if you are far enough away from a city to avoid the glare of its lights. Like their asteroid relatives, meteorites have different compositions—stony, metallic, and stony-iron.

Distance in the solar system

What is the farthest distance you have travelled? For most people, the answer will be in the hundreds or thousands of kilometers. Only a few people in human history can say their longest trip ever was in the hundreds of thousands of kilometers! To travel that far in a single trip, you have to leave Earth. The Apollo astronauts who visited the moon went more than 384,000 kilometers each way. They had to travel for three days to go that far!

People may visit Mars in the near future. The distance to Mars makes a trip to the moon seem quick and easy. At the closest point in its orbit to Earth, Mars is still more than 55 million kilometers away. The trip from Earth to Mars is expected to take one year or more.

It is important to remember that perceptions of size and distance are relative. While the distance from Earth to Mars is hard to envision, it is quite short when compared with the rest of outer space. While it takes our spacecraft about one year to travel from Earth to Mars, light can make the same trip in about seven minutes. Look at the data in the table about how far planets in our solar system typically are from the sun.

The closest planet to the sun—Mercury—is more than 145 times further from the sun than the moon is from Earth. With this in mind, does the moon feel a little bit closer than it did before?

Average Distance of Planets from the Sun

Planet	Distance from the Sun (in astronomical units)	Distance from the Sun (in millions of kilometers)
Mercury	0.387	56
Venus	0.722	108
Earth	1	150
Mars	1.52	229
Jupiter	5.20	779
Saturn	9.58	1431
Uranus	19.2	2881
Neptune	30.1	4506

A Light Year

Stars besides our sun are much farther away than the planets are. In fact, stars are so far away that a new unit of length—the light year—was developed to measure their distance. A light year is equal to the distance that light travels in one year. Since light travels at a velocity of about 3×10^8 m/s, one light year is equal to about 9.46 trillion kilometers!

The star closest to Earth—after the sun—is Proxima Centauri; it is more than 4 light years away. To walk an equivalent distance, a person would have to walk around the Earth more than 944 million times! Four space probes—Voyagers 1 and 2 and Pioneers 10 and 11—are en route to interstellar space, traveling at a rate of approximately 40,000 km/h. Even at this astounding speed, it would take 150,000 years for these probes to reach Proxima Centauri.

The light year is also helpful when describing the size of a galaxy. For example, the Milky Way galaxy is a disc-shaped spiral galaxy about 100,000 light years across and 1,000 light years thick. The farthest objects we can observe are more than 10 billion light years away. Although the stars may appear to be similar distances from Earth, these distances vary greatly.

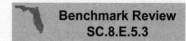

Our Galaxy and Beyond

A large group of stars and nebulae—giant clouds of dust and gas—bound together by gravity are called a **galaxy**. Galaxies come in a variety of sizes and shapes; the largest ones contain more than a trillion stars. Our solar system is located in the Milky Way galaxy, which looks like a spiral disk or a pancake with a central bulge. The sun is located on the spiral about two-thirds of the way out from the galactic core. The disk of the Milky Way is about 100,000 light-years across, and about 1,000 light-years thick.

Even the Milky Way can be considered small when looking at it from the context of the universe. The universe is composed of billions of galaxies, each containing billions of stars. Our galaxy barely registers if looking at the universe, and our sun and planets are only a small part of our galaxy.

Student-Response Activity

1 How do the sizes of planets, solar systems, galaxies, and the universe relate to one another?

_____

_____

_____

_____

_____

_____

2 What are some design limitations of making a scale model of the Milky Way galaxy?

_____

_____

_____

_____

_____

_____

Name ______________________________ Date ____________

Benchmark Review
SC.8.E.5.3

3 What do you notice about the size of the planets?

____
____
____
____
____
____

4 What is the difference between a comet and an asteroid?

____
____
____
____
____
____

5 How is a light year helpful when describing the the size of a galaxy? Provide an example.

____
____
____
____
____
____
____

Benchmark Assessment SC.8.E.5.3

Fill in the letter of the best choice.

1 The average distance from the Earth to the sun is about 149.6 x 10^6 km. Proxima Centauri, the nearest star is about 39.9 x 10^{12} km away. Which statement is the **most** accurate?

(A) The sun is many hundreds of times closer to Earth than it is to Proxima Centauri.

(B) The sun is many thousands of times closer to Earth than it is Proxima Centauri.

(C) The sun is many hundreds of times closer to Proxima Centauri than it is to Earth.

(D) The sun is many thousands of times closer to Proxima Centauri than it is to Earth.

2 The star Aldebaran is an orange giant star in the constellation Taurus, the bull. Aldebaran is the eye of the bull, and is about 65 light years away. What would happen if Aldebaran were to explode tonight?

(F) We would see the explosion before we hear it.

(G) We would see the explosion right away.

(H) We would see the explosion in 65 years.

(I) We would never be able to see the explosion.

3 Which correctly orders the relationship from least to greatest in size?

(A) galaxy, planet, solar system, universe

(B) planet, galaxy, universe, solar system

(C) universe, galaxy, solar system, planet

(D) planet, solar system, galaxy, universe

4 Lamar explained to his classmates that there are a very large number of galaxies in the universe. Which answer **best** describes how many galaxies there are in the universe?

(F) billions

(G) millions

(H) thousands

(I) hundreds of millions

5 How far is the sun from the center of the Milky Way?

(A) on the very edge of the disc

(B) half way from the galactic core to the edge of the disc

(C) in the center of the galaxy

(D) two-thirds from the galactic core to the edge of the disc

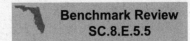
SC.8.E.5.5 Describe and classify specific physical properties of stars: apparent magnitude (brightness), temperature (color), size, and luminosity (absolute brightness).

What Are the Properties of Stars?

Why Are Some Stars Brighter Than Others?

A **star** is a large, celestial body made up of gas that produces its own light. While all stars have similar characteristics, there are a lot of differences in their specific physical properties. These properties include their apparent magnitude, temperature (color), size, and absolute brightness. In the night sky, some stars stand out more than others. These stars may be part of a constellation, or may just appear larger or brighter than other stars.

The first thing you may have noticed is the brightness of a star. The **apparent magnitude** is the measure of a star's brightness as seen from Earth. A star's apparent magnitude is measured on a scale using an inverse relationship, which means that the brighter an object appears, the lower its magnitude value is. A star's apparent magnitude is affected by its proximity to Earth. So, the closer a star is to Earth, the brighter it appears. Our sun is the closest star to Earth and appears very bright.

The temperature of stars varies and determines the color a star will appear. The electromagnetic spectrum is used to determine variance in the temperature of a star. Scientists use the color of light emitted from stars and from other celestial bodies to determine surface temperatures. Cooler objects emit red light. As an object becomes hotter, its color gradually changes from red to orange to white. So, stars that have relatively low surface temperatures are red or orange, and stars that have relatively high surface temperatures are white or blue. The sun is yellow, which falls in the middle of the spectrum.

Astronomers break a star's light into a spectrum that gives information about the composition and temperature of a star. When an element emits light, only some colors in the spectrum show up, while all the other colors are missing. Each element has a unique set of bright emission lines. Emission lines are lines that are made when certain wavelengths of light, or colors, are given off by hot gases.

The Sun

Stars have different sizes. Stars may be 1/100 as large as the sun or as much as 1,000 times as large as the sun. So what do astronomers use to measure star size? It is always easiest to start with an object that is familiar. That is why astronomers use the size of the sun to describe the size of other stars. Astronomers also compare star brightness. The **absolute brightness**, or luminosity, of a star is its *actual* brightness. A star's absolute brightness can be measured and compared against all other stars using a scale called **absolute magnitude**. This measurement is how bright a star would be if the star were located at a standard distance.

To understand the difference between apparent magnitude and absolute magnitude, let us use the sun as an example. The apparent magnitude of the sun is –26.8. However, the absolute magnitude of the sun is +4.8, which is typical of many stars. Now compare the sun, which is located 8.3 light-minutes from Earth, to Sirius, which is located 8.6 light-years from Earth. Sirius has an apparent magnitude of –1.46 and an absolute magnitude of +1.4.

Therefore, Sirius is much more luminous than the sun.

Magnitudes of Selected Stars			
Star	Distance from Earth	Apparent Magnitude	Absolute Magnitude
Sun	8.3 light-minutes	–26.8	+4.8
Sirius	8.6 light-years	–1.46	+1.4
Betelgeuse	640 light-years	+0.45	–5.6

The star that we are most familiar with is the

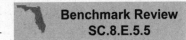

The Sun

The star that we are most familiar with is the sun. From Earth, the sun appears much larger and brighter than other stars; this is its apparent magnitude. The sun's absolute brightness is average among stars. The sun gives and sustains life on our planet. However, as we look at the physical properties of the sun, we find that it is not particularly large sized or high temperature; instead it is an average star. The sun, like other stars, is composed mostly of hydrogen and helium. The sun also contains oxygen, carbon, neon, and iron.

The sun rotates on its axis like other large bodies in the solar system. However, because the sun is a giant ball of gas, it does not rotate in the same way as a solid body like Earth does. Instead, the sun rotates faster at its equator than it does at higher latitudes. This kind of rotation is known as differential rotation. Differential rotation is the rotation of a body in which different parts of a body have different periods of rotation. Near the equator, the sun rotates once in about 25 days. However, at the poles, the sun rotates once in about 35 days.

Solar Activity

There is a lot of activity on the surface and inside of the sun. Dark areas that form on the surface of the sun are called **sunspots**. They are about 1,500 °C cooler than the areas that surround them. Sunspots are places where hot, convecting gases are prevented from reaching the sun's surface. **Solar flares** appear as very bright spots on the sun's photosphere. A **solar flare** is an explosive release of energy that can extend outward as far as the sun's outer atmosphere. During a solar flare, enormous numbers of high-energy particles are ejected at near the speed of light. Huge loops of relatively cool gas that extend outward from the photosphere thousands of kilometers into the outer atmosphere are called **prominences**. Several objects the size of Earth could fit inside a loop of a prominence. The gases in prominences are cooler than the surrounding atmosphere.

Student-Response Activity

❶ What does it mean if a star has a high absolute brightness and a low apparent magnitude?

_____

_____

_____

_____

_____

_____

_____

_____

Use the table to answer Questions 3 and 4.

Color and Surface Temperature of Stars	
Color	Surface Temperature (°C)
Blue	Above 25,000
blue-white	10,000–25,000
White	7,500–10,000
yellow-white	6,000–7,500
yellow	5,000–6,000
orange	3,500–5,000
red	Below 3,500

❸ Which stars have the highest surface temperatures, red stars or blue stars? Explain your answer.

_____

_____

_____

❹ How are a star's surface temperature and absolute brightness related?

_____

_____

_____

❺ Two flashlights are directed at a wall from different distances. The flashlights have the same strength of bulbs and of batteries. When the flashlights are turned on, which is expected to appear brighter on the wall? How does this analogy relate to stars?

_____

_____

_____

Benchmark Assessment SC.8.E.5.5

Fill in the letter of the best choice.

1 Which is **true** about the sun?

Ⓐ The sun is the largest star in the Milky Way galaxy.

Ⓑ The sun is the closest star to Earth in all galaxies.

Ⓒ The sun has the highest surface temperature of all stars in the Milky Way galaxy.

Ⓓ The sun has the highest absolute brightness of all stars in the Milky Way galaxy.

2 Why does a star, such as Betelgeuse, have a much greater absolute magnitude than apparent magnitude?

Magnitudes of Selected Stars			
Star	Distance from Earth	Apparent Magnitude	Absolute Magnitude
Sun	8.3 light-minutes	−26.8	+4.8
Sirius	8.6 light-years	−1.46	+1.4
Betelgeuse	640 light-years	+0.45	−5.6

Ⓕ Absolute magnitude is relative to the sun.

Ⓖ Apparent magnitude does not take into account the distance from Earth.

Ⓗ Absolute magnitude does not take into account the distance from Earth.

Ⓘ Betelgeuse is closer to Earth.

3 Which has the hottest temperature?

Ⓐ a blue star

Ⓑ a red giant star

Ⓒ the left over energy from the big bang

Ⓓ a swirling accretion disk of matter orbiting a black hole

4 An astronomer uses a telescope to observe a star. She observes that the color of this star is similar to the color of the sun. Therefore, she infers that the star and the sun have similar sizes and surface temperatures. Using this information, what can the astronomer conclude about the star?

Ⓕ The star is a white dwarf.

Ⓖ The star is cooler than a blue star.

Ⓗ The star is brighter than a red giant star.

Ⓘ The star is more distant than most other stars in our galaxy.

5 The sun does not rotate in the same way the Earth does. The sun has different periods of rotation at different latitudes. The figure below shows the rotation of the sun.

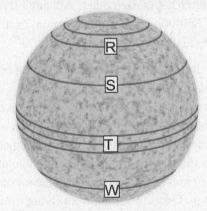

Which letter indicates the latitude at which the sun rotates the fastest?

Ⓐ R

Ⓑ S

Ⓒ T

Ⓓ W

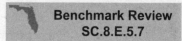
SC.8.E.5.7 Compare and contrast the properties of objects in the Solar System, including the Sun, planets, and moons to those of Earth, such as gravitational force, distance from the Sun, speed, movement, temperature, and atmospheric conditions.

Exploring the Solar System

Gravitational Force

Sir Isaac Newton explained the motions of the planets of the solar system at the same time that he described the force of gravity. Newton did not understand why gravity worked or what caused it. Even today, scientists do not fully understand gravity. But Newton combined the work of earlier scientists and used mathematics to explain the effects of gravity.

Newton reasoned that an object falls toward Earth because Earth and the object are attracted to each other by gravity. He discovered that this attraction depends on the masses of the objects and the distance between the objects. Both Earth and the moon are attracted to each other. Although it may seem as if Earth does not orbit the moon, Earth and the moon actually orbit each other.

Why does the moon not come crashing into Earth? The answer has to do with the moon's inertia. Inertia is an object's resistance to a change in speed or direction until an outside force acts on the object. In space, there is not any air to cause resistance and slow down the moving moon. Therefore, the moon continues to move, but gravity keeps the moon in its orbit. Gravity keeps the moon from flying off in a straight path. This principle holds true for all bodies in orbit, including Earth and other planets in our solar system as they orbit the sun.

Formation of the Solar System

Even though you do not feel it, gravity exists between all objects, regardless of how massive they are. While we are on Earth, we cannot detect the gravity of small objects very easily. This is similar to why you cannot see stars in the daytime. Earth's gravity is so strong that it overshadows the gravitational effects of smaller bodies. In outer space, however, even small objects attract each other with gravity.

Gravity can explain the formation of planets, stars, and solar systems. Billions of years ago, our Solar System was a spinning nebula of dust and gas. When small objects join together, so does the force of their gravity. As the particles became attracted to each other, they collected into large bodies. Gravity caused the central mass to further condense which caused it to heat up and begin to rotate faster. This is how scientists think the sun formed. The centrifugal force of the sun caused a disc-like shape to form. Gravity attracted the remaining gas and dust particles together to form planets, moons, and smaller objects that continue to orbit the sun.

Progression of Models

Various models and theories of the Solar System exist and are constantly evolving. For example, in 2006 our solar system downgraded from nine planets to eight, labeling Pluto as a dwarf planet. At one time, scientists used a geocentric model of our solar system. This model was first proposed by ancient Greek astronomers who placed Earth at the center of our Solar System, as shown in this diagram.

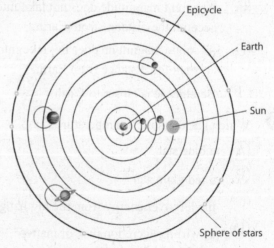

Ptolemy's Model

In 1543, a Polish scientist named Nicolaus Copernicus published a book that proposed a heliocentric model of our solar system. His model placed the sun at the center of the solar system, with all the planets orbiting it. Copernicus's model spread throughout the scientific world in Europe. Copernicus's model would prove to be the most controversial model that scientists had ever developed.

Our World

As viewed from space, Earth is like a sparkling blue oasis in a black sea of stars. Constantly changing weather patterns create the swirls of clouds that blanket the blue and brown sphere we call home. Why did Earth have such good fortune, while its two nearest neighbors, Venus and Mars, are unsuitable for life as we know it?

Earth formed at just the right distance from the sun. Earth is warm enough to keep most of its water from freezing. But unlike Venus, Earth is cool enough to keep its water from boiling away. Liquid water is a vital part of the chemical processes that living things depend on for survival.

Earth's mass also plays an important role because the mass "holds" the gases that constitute Earth's life-sustaining atmosphere around the Earth. The atmosphere is a mixture of gases that surrounds Earth. The atmosphere is approximately 78% nitrogen, 21% oxygen, and 1% argon, carbon dioxide, water vapor, and other gases. In addition to containing the oxygen you need to breathe, the atmosphere protects you from the sun's damaging rays.

Looking at the average surface temperatures shown in the table, many planets have extreme highs or lows regarding temperature. Earth's median position from the sun seems to make it more suitable for life than many other planets as the average temperature falls in the median range.

Planetary Data

Planet	Distance from the Sun (AU)	Gravity (m/s^2)	Average Surface Temperature (°C)	Atmosphere	Orbital Period (Earth years)
Mercury	0.39	3.7	260	Very thin, nearly undetectable	0.2408467
Venus	0.72	8.87	480	Thick	0.61519726
Earth	1.00	9.80665	15	Yes	1.0000174
Mars	1.52	3.71	−60	Thin layer	1.8808476
Jupiter	5.20	24.79	−150	Thick	11.862615
Saturn	9.58	10.4	−170	Thick	29.447498
Uranus	19.2	8.87	−200	Thick	84.016846
Neptune	30.05	11.15	−210	Thick	164.79132

Evidence of dried riverbeds has been found on other planets, showing that water has been present in the past on planets. This leads scientists to believe that changes may occur over time on celestial objects.

Student-Response Activity

1 How does a heliocentric model of the Solar System differ from a geocentric model?

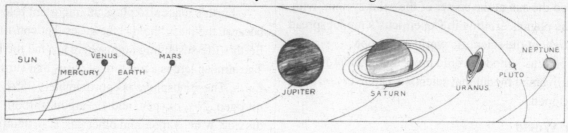

_____

_____

_____

_____

2 Use your own words to explain planetary gravitation. Provide an example.

_____

_____

_____

_____

3 Carlos states that planets that are closer to the sun have a higher surface temperature than those that are further from the sun. Why do you think Carlos is correct or incorrect?

_____

_____

_____

_____

4 Why are none of the outer planets likely to support life similar to that of Earth?

_____

_____

_____

_____

Benchmark Assessment SC.8.E.5.7

Fill in the letter of the best choice.

Use the table to answer Questions 1–4.

Planetary Data

Planet	Distance from the Sun (AU)	Gravity (m/s^2)	Average Surface Temperature (°C)	Atmosphere	Orbital Period (Earth years)
Mercury	0.39	3.7	260	Very thin, nearly undetectable	0.2408467
Venus	0.72	8.87	480	Thick	0.61519726
Earth	1.00	9.80665	15	Yes	1.0000174
Mars	1.52	3.71	−60	Thin layer	1.8808476
Jupiter	5.20	24.79	−150	Thick	11.862615
Saturn	9.58	10.4	−170	Thick	29.447498
Uranus	19.2	8.87	−200	Thick	84.016846
Neptune	30.05	11.15	−210	Thick	164.79132

1 Looking at the distances from the sun and the orbital period, which infers the relationship between these properties?

(A) As distances from the sun increase, the orbital period increases.

(B) As distances from the sun increase, the orbital period decreases.

(C) As distances from the sun decrease, the orbital period increases.

(D) There is no consistent relationship between the distances from the sun and the orbital period.

2 Which statement correctly compares the force of gravity between planets?

(F) The force of gravity on Mars is greater than the force of gravity on Uranus.

(G) The force of gravity on Earth is greater than the force of gravity on Jupiter.

(H) The force of gravity on Saturn is equal to the force of gravity on Neptune.

(I) The force of gravity on Venus is equal to the force of gravity on Uranus.

3 Based on the information given, which inference can be drawn?

(A) Presence of an atmosphere determines the presence of life.

(B) Presence of an atmosphere does not determine the presence of life.

(C) The atmosphere of a planet becomes thicker as it is a further distance from Earth.

(D) The atmosphere of a planet becomes thicker as it is a further distance from the sun.

4 Which orders the orbital period, from least to greatest?

(F) Earth, Mercury, Mars, Uranus

(G) Mercury, Earth, Mars, Uranus

(H) Mars, Mercury, Earth, Uranus

(I) Uranus, Mars, Earth, Mercury

SC.8.E.5.9 Explain the impact of objects in space on each other, including:
1. the Sun on the Earth, including seasons and gravitational attraction:
2. the Moon on the Earth, including phases, tides, and eclipses, and the relative position of each body.

The Earth-Moon-Sun System

Earth's Movement

Earth experiences two types of motion. Earth rotates in a counterclockwise motion around its axis much like a spinning toy top. The spinning of a body, such as a planet, is called **rotation**. As a location on Earth rotates from west to east, the stars appear to rise in the east. The stars then appear to have moved across the sky to the west.

As Earth rotates, only one-half faces the sun. People on the half of Earth facing the sun experience daylight, or daytime. At the same time, the half of Earth that faces away from the sun experiences darkness, or nighttime. Earth's rotation is used to measure time. Earth completes one rotation in 24 hours, or in one day.

As Earth rotates on its axis, it also revolves around the sun. The motion of a body that travels around another body in space is called **revolution**. Earth completes one revolution around the sun in about one year. Earth's orbit around the sun and the tilt of its axis at 23.5° cause the seasonal changes experienced in most locations on Earth. This tilt affects how much solar energy an area receives as Earth moves around the sun. It is important to note that Earth maintains the 23.5° tilt as it orbits the sun, therefore its axis is pointing toward the North Star, also known as Polaris, at all times during its yearly revolution around the sun.

Some places on Earth do not experience seasonal changes. For example, places close to the equator have approximately the same temperatures and same amount of daylight year-round.

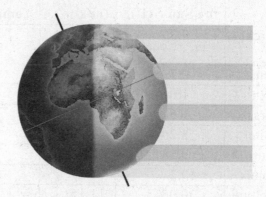

Latitude and the tilt of Earth determine the seasons and the length of the day in a particular area. During summer in the Northern Hemisphere, locations experience warmer temperatures and a greater number of daylight hours because this hemisphere tilts toward the sun and receives more direct solar energy. At the same time, the Southern Hemisphere has colder temperatures and fewer daylight hours because it is tilted away from the sun and receives much less concentrated solar energy. During winter in the Northern Hemisphere, the Southern Hemisphere has higher temperatures and a greater number of daylight hours because it is tilted toward the sun and receives more direct solar energy. At that time, the Northern Hemisphere has lower temperatures and fewer daylight hours because it is tilted away from the sun and receives much less concentrated solar energy. The illustration above shows Earth's position during winter in the Northern Hemisphere. The Northern Hemisphere receives much less direct solar energy because the sunlight is spread out over a larger area.

Moon Phases

One of the most noticeable aspects of the moon is its continually changing appearance. Over the course of one month, the moon's appearance changes from a fully lit circle, to a thin crescent, and

back to a circle. These differences in the moon's appearance, called phases, result from how its position changes in relation to Earth and the sun. As the moon revolves around Earth, the amount of sunlight on its Earth-facing side changes. When the moon is waxing, the sunlit fraction that we can see from Earth gets larger. When the moon is waning, the sunlit fraction gets smaller. Even as the moon's phases change, the total amount of sunlight the moon gets remains the same. One-half of the moon is always in sunlight, but because the moon's period of rotation is the same as its period of revolution, we always see the same side of the moon. If you lived on the far side of the moon, you would see the sun for one-half of each lunar day, but never Earth!

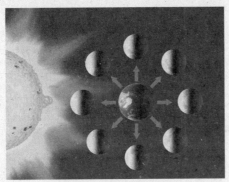

Phases of the Moon

Eclipses

As Earth and the moon move around the sun, they will align in such a way as to cause an eclipse. An **eclipse** is an event during which one object in space casts a shadow onto another. There are two types of eclipses—a lunar eclipse and a solar eclipse. A lunar eclipse occurs when the moon moves through Earth's shadow and causes Earth to block the sun's light from reaching the moon. A lunar eclipse takes place during a full moon. During a solar eclipse, the moon blocks the sun's light from reaching Earth. The moon's shadow is cast on Earth, which causes it to get dark during the daytime.

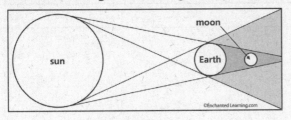

Lunar Eclipse

Solar Eclipse

Tides

Tides are daily changes in the level of ocean water. Tides are caused by the difference in the gravitational force of the sun and moon across Earth. This difference in gravitational force is called tidal force. Because the moon is closer to Earth, the tidal force exerted by it is stronger than the tidal force exerted by the sun.

The moon's gravitational pull decreases with the moon's distance from Earth. The part of Earth facing the moon is pulled toward it with the greatest force, which causes water on that side of Earth to bulge toward the moon. The gravitational pull occurs simultaneously on the opposite side of Earth, due to the combined motions of Earth and the moon that "throw" or push water to the side opposite the moon as Earth spins. The bulges that form in Earth's oceans are called high tides; as water moves outward into the bulges, low places, called low tides, are also formed. As the moon moves around Earth and Earth rotates, these bulges follow the motion of the moon. As a result, many places on Earth have two high tides and two low tides each day. Because Earth rotates more rapidly than the moon circles around Earth, the locations of high tides constantly change.

The sun is farther away from Earth, so its gravitational influence is less. However, during full and new moons that take place every 14 days, or twice a month, the sun, Earth, and the moon are all lined up and cause spring tides to occur. Spring tides have the greatest variation and are the highest of high tides and lowest of low tides. Seven days after full or new moons, the sun, Earth, and the moon form a 90-degree angle, causing neap tides to occur. Neap tides vary the least in a daily cycle.

Name ______________________ Date __________

Benchmark Review
SC.8.E.5.9

Student-Response Activity

1. Why does the moon have a greater effect on tidal change than the sun?

2. How does the tilt of Earth's axis affect seasons?

3. Why is only one side of the moon visible from Earth?

4. What is the relationship between Earth, the sun, and the moon in space?

5. How would the tides on Earth be different if the moon revolved around Earth in 15 days instead of 30 days?

6. How do the tilt of Earth's axis and Earth's movements around the sun cause seasons?

Benchmark Assessment SC.8.E.5.9

Fill in the letter of the best choice.

1 Maria lives in Miami, Florida, where the weather is very warm most of the year. Her grandparents live in Canada where they have very cold winters. Which **best** explains why the seasons are so different between Maria's house and her grandparents?

(A) Parts of Earth closer to the equator do not experience as many seasonal changes.

(B) Parts of Earth closer to the equator receive indirect rays from the sun all year long.

(C) Parts of Earth farther away from the equator do not experience many seasonal changes.

(D) Parts of Earth farther away from the equator receive indirect rays from the sun all year long.

2 This diagram shows Earth's orbit. At what position is it autumn in the Southern Hemisphere?

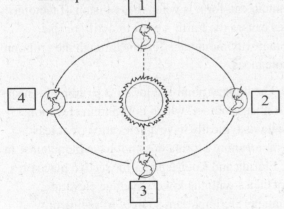

(F) Position 1
(G) Position 2
(H) Position 3
(I) Position 4

3 This diagram shows the positions of the sun, Earth, and the moon at neap tide. Which areas experience low tides when the sun, Earth, and the moon are arranged in these positions?

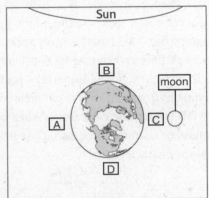

(A) A and C
(B) A and D
(C) B and C
(D) B and D

4 Which correctly describes the impact of a lunar eclipse?

(F) The Earth casts a shadow on the sun.
(G) The Earth casts a shadow on the moon.
(H) The moon casts a shadow on the sun.
(I) The moon casts a shadow on the Earth.

5 Why do moon phases repeat about every 28 days?

(A) The period of rotation of the moon is the same as its period of revolution.

(B) The moon takes about 28 days to revolve around the Earth.

(C) Twenty-eight days is the period of a complete cycle of tides.

(D) Cloud-cover patterns on Earth last 28 days.

SC.7.E.6.2 Identify the patterns within the rock cycle and relate them to surface events (weathering and erosion) and subsurface events (plate tectonics and mountain building).

The Rock Cycle

Types of Rock

The **rock cycle** is a series of processes in which rock changes from one type to another. The three main classes of rock—sedimentary, igneous, and metamorphic—are based on how rocks form. **Igneous rock** forms when magma cools and hardens to become solid. **Sedimentary rock** forms when sediment from older rocks get pressed together. **Metamorphic rock** forms when pressure, temperature, or chemical processes change a rock's structure and characteristics.

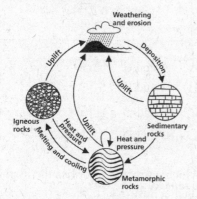

Weathering, Erosion, and Deposition

Weathering, erosion, and deposition are natural processes that change the environment. **Weathering** is a process by which water, wind, ice, and changes in temperature break down rock into smaller pieces called sediment. For example, limestone is a common type of rock formed by weathering. Limestone has tiny spaces within it that can hold groundwater. This groundwater dissolves the limestone over time to form caves.

Erosion is the process by which sediment is moved from one place to another. Water, ice, wind, and gravity all can erode sediment to deposit somewhere else. This depositing, or laying down, of material is called **deposition**. For example, when a river is no longer flowing quickly enough to carry larger, heavier pieces of sediment, the pieces drop onto the bottom. That is, the sediment is deposited.

The processes of weathering, erosion, and deposition continually shape the ecoregions of Florida. For example, frequent winds and continuous ocean waves erode and deposit sediment along the Gulf Coast of Florida. These processes also reshape islands off the coast by eroding materials and depositing them elsewhere. Wind and water deposit large amounts of sand that are called sand dunes. Over time winds blow through areas of sand dunes, causing the dunes to change shape. Tropical storms and hurricanes can greatly impact the coastline of Florida in a short period of time. Rain and snow can wash away parts of rock. Rivers can cause mountains to erode by washing away sediment. Rivers can branch into deltas when they reach a coastline. Glaciers are large sheets of ice that cover land and as they move, erode the land.

Landforms

A mountain is a region of increased elevation on Earth's surface that rises to a peak. One way a mountain can form is when the collision of tectonic plates causes the Earth's crust to uplift, or rise. Another way mountains form is through the eruption of volcanoes.

The highest point in Florida is Britton Hill near the Alabama border, which is 105 m in elevation. Mountains typically have an elevation of at least 300 m, meaning Florida does not have mountains! In fact, Florida and Louisiana tie for second place on a list of states with the lowest average elevation. Mountains are important sources of sediment. Sediment refers to any pieces of rock that have been broken down from existing rock over time. Sediments can be transported to new locations. For example, sediment from the Appalachian Mountains is continually being transported to areas including Florida. In fact, millions of years ago these sediments formed layers of sedimentary rock, which helped build up the land that is Florida today.

How can mountains get broken down into sediments? One method is through the action of glaciers. A glacier is a mass of gradually moving or flowing ice. As snow and ice build on a mountain, the glacier can begin to move down the mountain. Glaciers scrape and relocate rocks as they move, forming sediments. Glaciers can be found at high elevations and near Earth's poles. An ice sheet is a very large glacier that covers a large area. Approximately 18,000 years ago, much of Canada and the northern portion of the United States were covered by an ice sheet. During this glacial period, the sea level on Earth was reduced as the water was stored in the ice. As a result, the land area of Florida was much larger than it is today. Once the ice sheet began to melt, sediments were deposited throughout the United States. In addition, the sea level rose again, altering Florida's shape and size.

A lake is a body of fresh or salt water that is surrounded by land. Streams and rivers that carry water and sediment feed lakes. Many of the lakes in Florida are sinkhole lakes. A sinkhole is a hole in the ground caused by the collapse of an underground cavern. Often, sinkholes become plugged by sediments and later get filled by water, forming sinkhole lakes. Florida has approximately 30,000 lakes of varying size.

Rivers are one method of transporting sediment. A river is a large, natural stream of water that flows into an ocean or other large body of water, such as a lake. Rivers start as smaller flowing bodies of water, called streams, at higher elevations. The streams can combine to eventually form rivers that flow along a channel. In Florida, most of the rivers are relatively short and do not flow quickly because of the flat elevation of the state.

When a river reaches a lake, ocean, or other body of water, the sediments carried in a river can form a delta. A delta is a deposit, formed by sediment that accumulates at the mouth of a river. Most of Florida's rivers carry a limited amount of sediment and do not flow very fast. Therefore, Florida rivers do not form large or significant deltas. An exception to this is the Apalachicola River in the Florida Panhandle. The river is part of a larger river system that begins in the Appalachian Mountains and ends in the Florida Panhandle. Sediments are carried in the river and deposited into the Gulf of Mexico, forming deltas.

Florida has a long coastline. A coastline is a dynamic boundary between land and the ocean. Coastlines can vary from rocky coasts with high, sharp cliffs, to gently-sloping sandy beaches. A number of factors control the characteristics of coastlines including waves, wind, sediment supply, tides, and the geology of the region.

Human Impact

Human activities can have positive and negative effects on land and soil. Some activities restore land to its natural state, or increase the amount of fertile soil on land. Other activities can degrade land. Urbanization, deforestation, and poor farming practices can all lead to land degradation.

When too many livestock are kept in one area, they can overgraze the area. Overgrazing removes the plants and roots that hold topsoil together. Overgrazing and other poor farming methods can cause desertification. Desertification is the process by which land becomes more desert like and unable to support life. Without plants, soil becomes dusty and prone to wind erosion. Deforestation and urbanization can also lead to desertification.

The removal of trees and other vegetation from an area is called deforestation. Logging for wood can cause deforestation. Surface mining causes deforestation by removing vegetation and soil to get to the minerals below. Deforestation also occurs in rainforests when farmers cut or burn down trees so they can grow crops. Urbanization can cause deforestation when forests are replaced with buildings. Deforestation leads to increased soil erosion.

Student-Response Activity

1 How are sediments created and how do those sediments make new landforms?

_____
_____
_____

2 Use an example to describe how deposition changes Earth's surface.

_____
_____
_____

3 Complete the cause-and-effect graphic organizer below.

Cause: Glaciers cover

land and move slowly.

Effect: _____

_____

_____

_____

_____

4 Identify all features of Earth's surface shown here.

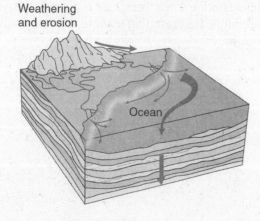

_____
_____
_____
_____
_____
_____
_____

5 Complete the Venn diagram to compare and contrast weathering and erosion.

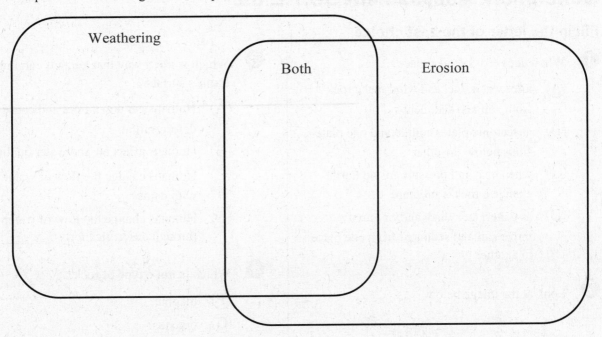

Weathering

Both

Erosion

6 How might deforestation lead to desertification?

_____

_____

_____

_____

_____

_____

Benchmark Assessment SC.7.E.6.2

Fill in the letter of the best choice.

1 When does erosion take place?

Ⓐ after water, ice, and wind make rock from soil and sediment

Ⓑ as tectonic plates collide and one plate sinks below the other

Ⓒ when heat and pressure inside Earth change a rock's structure

Ⓓ as water, ice, wind, and/or gravity move soil and sediment from one place to another

2 Look at the image below.

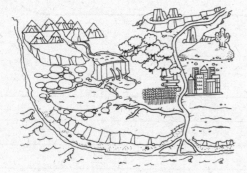

How does the river change the land?

Ⓕ The river builds up the mountains by depositing sand.

Ⓖ The river erodes the mountains by washing away sediment.

Ⓗ The river forces magma to Earth's surface.

Ⓘ The river changes rock with heat and pressure.

3 Which is **not** a way that humans can impact Earth's surface?

Ⓐ Humans cut down trees and cause deforestation.

Ⓑ Humans affect air and water quality.

Ⓒ Humans change the flow of water with dams.

Ⓓ Humans change the flow of water through desertification.

4 Which is **not** a type of rock?

Ⓕ magma

Ⓖ igneous

Ⓗ sedimentary

Ⓘ metamorphic

5 Look at the drawing below.

Which prediction is correct?

Ⓐ Over time, the rock will become a metamorphic rock.

Ⓑ Over time, the rock will become an igneous rock.

Ⓒ Over time, the rock will become a sedimentary rock.

Ⓓ Over time, the rock will become magma.

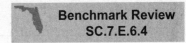
SC.7.E.6.4 Explain and give examples of how physical evidence supports scientific theories that Earth has evolved over geologic time due to natural processes.

Earth's Evolution Over Time

Sedimentary Rock

How does sedimentary rock show Earth's history? Rock and mineral fragments move from one place to another during erosion. Eventually, this sediment is deposited in layers. As new layers of sediment are deposited, they cover older layers. Older layers become compacted. Dissolved minerals, such as calcite and quartz, separate from water that passes through the sediment. This forms a natural cement that holds the rock and mineral fragments together in sedimentary rock.

The composition of sedimentary rock shows the source of the sediment that makes up the rock. Some sedimentary rock forms when rock or mineral fragments are cemented together. Sandstone forms when sand grains are deposited and buried, then cemented together. Other sedimentary rock forms from the remains of once-living plants and animals. Most limestone forms from the remains of animals that lived in the ocean. Another sedimentary rock, called coal, forms underground from partially decomposed plant material that is buried beneath sediment.

The texture of sedimentary rock shows the environment in which the sediment was carried and deposited. Sedimentary rock is arranged in layers. Layers can differ from one another, depending on the kind, size, and color of their sediment. Features on sedimentary rock called ripple marks record the motion of wind or water waves over sediment. Other features, called mud cracks, form when fine-grained sediments at the bottom of a shallow body of water are exposed to the air and dry out. Mud cracks show that an ancient lake, stream, or ocean shoreline was once a part of an area.

Earth's Changing Surface

The continents have been moving throughout Earth's history. For example, at one time the continents formed a single landmass called Pangaea. Pangaea broke apart about 200 million years ago. Since then, the continents have been slowly moving to their present locations, and continue to move today. Evidence of Pangaea can be seen by the way rock types, mountains, and fossils are now distributed on Earth's surface. For example, mountain-building events from tectonic plate movements produced different mountain belts on Earth.

The movement of tectonic plates across Earth has resulted in extraordinary events. When continental plates collide, mountain ranges can form. As they pull apart, magma can be released in volcanic eruptions. When they grind past one another, breaks in Earth's surface form, where earthquakes can occur. Collisions between oceanic and continental plates can also cause volcanoes and the formation of mountains.

In addition to forces that build up Earth's surface features, there are forces that break them down as well. Weathering and erosion always act on Earth's surface, changing it with time. For example, high, jagged mountains can become lower and more rounded over time. So, the height and shape of mountains can tell scientists about the geologic history of mountains.

Measuring the Age of Earth

Sedimentary rock can contain fossils. A fossil is a record of an organism that has been preserved in the rock. Fossils may be skeletons or body parts, shells, burrows, or ancient coral reefs. Fossils form in many different ways. Some fossils formed when organisms became trapped in amber or asphalt. Others formed when organisms were buried in rock, became frozen or petrified.

Because sedimentary rock forms from particles of sediment compressed together, the layers of rock on the bottom are the oldest layers, and the layers on top are the youngest layers. This is called the law of superposition. This means that the oldest fossils are in the bottom layers of sedimentary rock. Fossils in the top layers are from more recent organisms. Scientists can use this knowledge to determine when different animals and plants lived relative to one another.

Supporting Scientific Theories —Radioactive Dating

New radioactive dating methods show that rocks in corresponding parts of Africa and South America formed at the same time, thus supporting plate tectonics. The dating of igneous rocks around mid-ocean ridges showed a symmetrical pattern, in which older rocks were located farther away from the ridge. Few rocks older than 180 million years were discovered on the ocean floor. This discovery indicates that the oceanic lithosphere is continuously recycled.

Radioactive dating is one way scientists can determine the age of fossils and rock samples. Some radioactive elements decay at known rates. For example, carbon 14 is a radioactive carbon isotope that decays over several thousand years. The proportion of carbon 14 in a fossil or rock tells how old the fossil or rock is. A rock with a large proportion of carbon 14 is younger because most of its carbon 14 has not decayed yet. A rock with less carbon 14 is older because more of the carbon 14 has decayed.

Student-Response Activity

1 A fossil has very little carbon 14. What does this tell you about the fossil? Explain your reasoning.

_____

_____

_____

_____

_____

_____

Name ______________________ Date __________

Benchmark Review
SC.7.E.6.4

❷ One fossil is in a layer of rock on top of another fossil. What does this tell you about the relative ages of the fossils?

❸ Write two ways that natural processes change Earth over time.

❹ Explain how the law of superposition and radioactive dating support scientific theories that Earth has evolved over geologic time due to natural processes.

❺ Suppose a fossil was buried thousands of years ago. Describe how the fossil changed over time and how scientists can determine the age of the fossil.

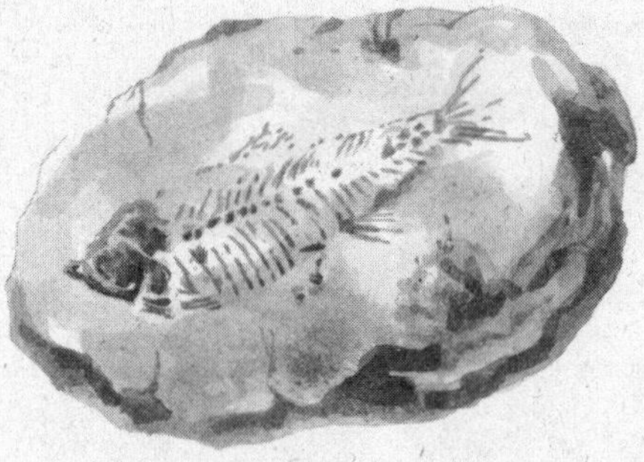

Benchmark Assessment SC.7.E.6.4

Fill in the letter of the best choice.

1 Which statement is **true** according to the law of superposition?

- (A) Young fossils replace old fossils.
- (B) Oldest fossils are in the top rock layers.
- (C) Oldest fossils are in the bottom rock layers.
- (D) Youngest fossils are in the bottom rock layers.

2 Which method do scientists use to find the *relative* ages of rock samples?

- (F) law of superposition
- (G) law of relative ages
- (H) radioactive dating
- (I) carbon 14 dating

3 Examine the image shown below.

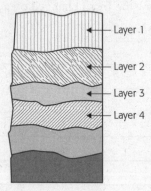

Which letter represents the youngest layer of rock?

- (A) Layer 1
- (B) Layer 2
- (C) Layer 3
- (D) Layer 4

4 How can scientists use carbon 14 to determine the age of a rock?

- (F) Rocks that have more carbon 14 are older.
- (G) Only rocks from a certain time period contain carbon 14.
- (H) Because carbon 14 does not decay, it shows the rock's age.
- (I) The proportion of carbon 14 in the rock tells how old it is.

5 A rock formation near Gainesville, Florida, was formed 530 million years ago. Which information does a scientist need to **most accurately** determine the age of a rock?

- (A) the percentage of mineral that makes up the rock
- (B) the percentage of fossilized marine life that makes up the rock
- (C) the amount of each radioactive element present in the rock
- (D) the amount of weathering present on the surface of the rock

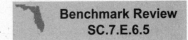
SC.7.E.6.5 Explore the scientific theory of plate tectonics by describing how the movement of Earth's crustal plates causes both slow and rapid changes in Earth's surface, including volcanic eruptions, earthquakes, and mountain building.

The Structures of Earth

Earth's Layers

The Earth is divided into three layers—the crust, the mantle, and the core—based on the chemical composition of each one. The outermost solid layer of Earth is the crust. There are two types of crust—continental and oceanic. Both types are made mainly of the elements oxygen, silicon, and aluminum. However, the denser oceanic crust has almost twice as much iron, calcium, and magnesium. These elements form minerals that are denser than those in the continental crust.

The mantle is located between the core and the crust. It is a region of hot, slow-flowing, solid rock. When convection takes place in the mantle, cooler rock sinks and warmer rock rises. Convection is the movement of matter that results from differences in density caused by variations in temperature. Scientists can learn about the mantle by observing mantle rock that has risen to Earth's surface. The mantle is denser than the crust. It contains more magnesium and less aluminum and silicon than the crust does.

The core extends from below the mantle to the center of Earth. Scientists think that the core is made mostly of iron and some nickel. Scientists also think that it contains much less oxygen, silicon, aluminum, and magnesium than the mantle does. The core is the densest layer. It makes up about one-third of Earth's mass.

Earth can also be divided into five layers depending on its physical, or structural, characteristics. Starting from Earth's center, the physical layers are the inner core, outer core, mesosphere, asthenosphere, and lithosphere. The inner core is the solid, dense center of our planet that extends from the bottom of the outer core to the center of Earth, which is about 6,380 km beneath the surface. The outer core is the liquid layer of Earth's core. It lies beneath the

mantle and surrounds the inner core. The strong, lower part of the mantle is called the mesosphere. Rock in the mesosphere flows more slowly than rock in the asthenosphere does. The asthenosphere is a layer of weak or soft mantle that is made of rock that flows slowly. Tectonic plates move on top of this layer. The outermost, rigid layer of Earth is the lithosphere. The lithosphere is made of two parts—the crust and the rigid, upper part of the mantle. The lithosphere is divided into pieces called tectonic plates.

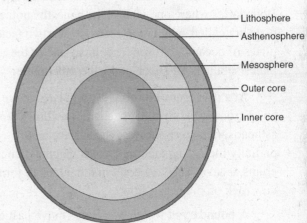

Lithosphere
Asthenosphere
Mesosphere
Outer core
Inner core

What Is Plate Tectonics?

Plate tectonics is a theory that describes the large-scale movements of Earth's lithosphere. It describes why and how Earth's continents move and explains the formation of features in Earth's crust. The **lithosphere,** or the solid outer layer of Earth, is divided into tectonic plates that move in different directions and different speeds. Each plate fits together with the plates surrounding it. The plates all vary in size, shape, and thickness.

Plate Boundaries

A **plate boundary** is where two tectonic plates meet. The most dramatic changes in Earth's crust occur along plate boundaries. Plate boundaries may be on the ocean floor, around the edges of continents, or even within continents. There are three types of plate boundaries: convergent boundaries, divergent boundaries, and transform boundaries. Each type of plate boundary is associated with characteristic landforms.

Convergent boundaries form where two plates collide. Three types of collisions can happen at convergent boundaries. When two tectonic plates of continental lithosphere collide, they buckle and thicken, which pushes some of the continental crust upward. When a plate of oceanic lithosphere collides with a plate of continental lithosphere, the denser oceanic lithosphere sinks into the asthenosphere. Boundaries where one plate sinks beneath another plate are called subduction zones. When two tectonic plates of oceanic lithosphere collide, one of the plates subducts, or sinks, under the other plate.

At a **divergent boundary**, two plates move away from each other. This separation allows the asthenosphere to rise toward the surface and partially melt. This melting creates magma, which erupts as lava. The lava cools and hardens to form new rock on the ocean floor.

A boundary at which two plates move past each other horizontally is called a **transform boundary**. However, the plate edges do not slide along smoothly. Instead, they scrape against each other in a series of sudden slippages of crustal rock that are felt as earthquakes. Unlike other types of boundaries, transform boundaries generally do not produce magma. The San Andreas Fault in California is a major transform boundary between the North American plate and the Pacific plate. Transform motion also occurs at divergent boundaries. Short segments of mid-ocean ridges are connected by transform faults called fracture zones.

Why Plates Move

Scientists have proposed three mechanisms to explain how tectonic plates move over Earth's surface. Mantle convection drags plates along as mantle material moves beneath tectonic plates. Ridge push moves plates away from mid-ocean ridges as rock cools and becomes denser. Slab pull tugs plates along as the dense edge of a plate sinks beneath Earth's surface.

As atoms in Earth's core and mantle undergo radioactive decay, energy is released as heat. Some parts of the mantle become hotter than other parts. The hot parts rise as the sinking of cooler, denser material pushes the heated material up. This kind of movement of material due to differences in density is called convection. It was thought that as the mantle convects, or moves, it would drag the overlying tectonic plates along with it. However, many scientists have criticized this hypothesis because it does not explain the huge amount of force that would be needed to move plates.

Newly formed rock at a mid-ocean ridge is warm and less dense than older, adjacent rock. Because of its lower density, the new rock rests at a higher elevation than the older rock. The older rock slopes downward away from the ridge. As the newer, warmer rock cools, it also becomes denser. These cooling and increasingly dense rocks respond to gravity by moving down the slope of the asthenosphere, away from the ridge. This force, called ridge push, pushes the rest of the plate away from the mid-ocean ridge.

At subduction zones, a denser tectonic plate sinks, or subducts, beneath another, less dense plate. The leading edge of the subducting plate is colder and denser than the mantle. As it sinks, the leading edge of the plate pulls the rest of the plate with it. This process is called slab pull. In general, subducting plates move faster than other plates do. This evidence leads many scientists to think that slab pull may be the most important mechanism driving tectonic plate motion.

Mountains

The movement of energy as heat and material in Earth's interior contribute to tectonic plate motions that result in mountain building. Mountains can form through folding, volcanism, and faulting.

Folded mountains form when rock layers are squeezed together and pushed upward. They usually form at convergent boundaries, where plates collide. For example, the Appalachian Mountains formed from folding and faulting when the North American Plate collided with the Eurasian and African plates millions of years ago.

Volcanic mountains form when melted rock erupts onto Earth's surface. Many major volcanic mountains are located at convergent boundaries. Volcanic mountains can form on land or on the ocean floor. Volcanoes on the ocean floor can grow so tall that they rise above the surface of the ocean, forming islands. Most of Earth's active volcanoes are concentrated around the edge of the Pacific Ocean. This area is known as the Ring of Fire.

Fault-block mountains form when tension makes the lithosphere break into many normal faults. Along the faults, pieces of the lithosphere drop down compared with other pieces. The pieces left standing form fault-block mountains.

Volcanic Eruptions

Volcanic eruptions also occur when an oceanic plate sinks under a continental plate. The eruptions build up mountain ranges on the continental plate, near the plate boundary. If two continental plates converge, neither plate sinks, but instead they push against each other, causing Earth's surface to push up and form mountain ranges.

Earthquakes

Earthquakes are another kind of rapid change that occurs on Earth's surface. When two plates are moving apart, Earth's outer layer is stretched, and tension breaks the crust, forming large cracks called faults. This motion breaks and bends rock. Rock can become stuck as the plates scrape along. When the rocks that are stuck break free, energy is released. This makes Earth's surface shake—it causes an earthquake to occur.

Types of Faults

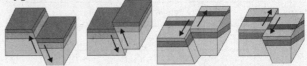

Earthquakes can occur at all plate boundaries. Fault-block mountains and valleys form as plate motion causes rock to move up or down on either side of a fault. Volcanism also occurs at these boundaries as rock melts below the thinning surface. This can form volcanic mountains.

Name ______________________ Date __________

Benchmark Review
SC.7.E.6.5

Student-Response Activity

❶ How does the mantle affect Earth's crust?

❷ Suppose two tectonic plates are colliding. What prediction can you make about how Earth's surface might change rapidly? How it might change slowly?

❸ How do folded, volcanic, and fault-block mountains differ?

❹ Identify each layer of Earth as a *solid* or a *liquid*.

crust ______________________

mantle ______________________

outer core ______________________

inner core ______________________

Benchmark Assessment SC.7.E.6.5

Fill in the letter of the best choice.

1 Which is **not** one of Earth's layers?

Ⓐ crust

Ⓑ inner core

Ⓒ mantle

Ⓓ ocean

2 Which layer extends from below the mantle to the center of Earth?

Ⓕ core

Ⓖ continental crust

Ⓗ lithosphere

Ⓘ oceanic core

3 Javier is going to construct a physical model of Earth. What is the correct order, from inside to outside, of Earth's layers?

Ⓐ crust, mantle, outer core, inner core

Ⓑ inner core, outer core, crust, mantle

Ⓒ inner core, outer core, mesosphere, asthenosphere, and lithosphere

Ⓓ lithosphere, asthenosphere, mesosphere, outer core, and inner core

4 Examine the diagram shown below.

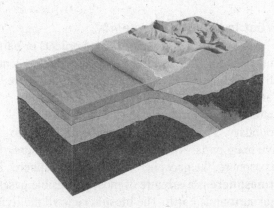

What does this diagram show?

Ⓕ tectonic plates pulling apart and forming mountains

Ⓖ tectonic plates colliding and causing an earthquake

Ⓗ tectonic plates causing a volcanic eruption

Ⓘ one tectonic plate sinking beneath another, forming mountains

5 Which is **not** explained by plate tectonics?

Ⓐ earthquakes

Ⓑ floods

Ⓒ mountain building

Ⓓ volcanoes

SC.6.E.7.4 Differentiate and show interactions among the geosphere, hydrosphere, cryosphere, atmosphere, and biosphere.

Earth's Spheres

What Is the Earth System?

A system is a group of related objects or parts that work together to form a whole. From the center of the planet to the outer edge of the atmosphere, Earth is a system. The **Earth system** is all the matter, energy, and processes within Earth's boundary. The Earth system can be divided into five main parts—the atmosphere, the biosphere, the cryosphere, the geosphere, and the hydrosphere. The **atmosphere** is a mixture of mostly invisible gases that surrounds Earth. The **biosphere** is all the living things on Earth, including plants, humans, and other animals. The **cryosphere** is all the frozen water on Earth, such as snow, ice, glaciers, sea ice, and ice shelves. The **geosphere** is the mostly solid, rocky part of Earth that extends from the center of Earth to its surface. The **hydrosphere** is all the liquid water on Earth, including oceans, rivers, and lakes.

The Geosphere

The geosphere is the solid, non-living matter on Earth. It includes the ground under your feet, the mountains that tower above the ground, and the rocks buried deep within Earth's interior. The geosphere is divided into three layers—the crust, the mantle, and the core. The crust is the thin, outermost layer of the geosphere. The crust is divided into plates that move slowly over Earth's surface; it is the layer you stand on. Beneath the crust is the mantle, which is made of molten rock. This layer is about 2900 km thick. Below the mantle is Earth's core, which is composed of iron and nickel and is very dense.

The Hydrosphere

In addition to saltwater found in the oceans, Earth's hydrosphere also includes the water in lakes, rivers, and marshes. Clouds and rain are also part of the hydrosphere. Even water underground is part of the hydrosphere. The hydrosphere connects all of Earth's spheres through a process called the water cycle. The water cycle is the continuous movement of water through evaporation, condensation,

precipitation, and runoff. Water from lakes, rivers, and the ocean evaporates into the atmosphere. In the atmosphere, the water cools and condenses to form clouds. Water falls from clouds as precipitation back to Earth's surface and collects in bodies of water again. Precipitation can be frozen snow, sleet, or hail, which are all parts of the cryosphere.

Sometimes glaciers or other parts of the cryosphere melt and collect in bodies of water. This water also evaporates into the atmosphere. Falling rain can cause weathering, or the wearing away of rock, in the geosphere. Precipitation can affect growing plants in the biosphere as living things take in and release water.

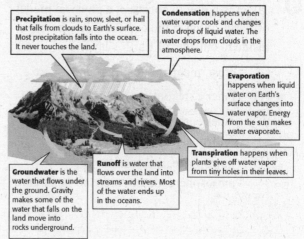

Precipitation is rain, snow, sleet, or hail that falls from clouds to Earth's surface. Most precipitation falls into the ocean. It never touches the land.

Condensation happens when water vapor cools and changes into drops of liquid water. The water drops form clouds in the atmosphere.

Evaporation happens when liquid water on Earth's surface changes into water vapor. Energy from the sun makes water evaporate.

Transpiration happens when plants give off water vapor from tiny holes in their leaves.

Runoff is water that flows over the land into streams and rivers. Most of the water ends up in the oceans.

Groundwater is the water that flows under the ground. Gravity makes some of the water that falls on the land move into rocks underground.

The Cryosphere

As all frozen forms of water are part of the cryosphere, it is closely related to the hydrosphere. Precipitation which falls on mountaintops as snow or ice can also form glaciers. The amount of frozen water in most of these areas often changes with the seasons. These changes, in turn, play an important role in Earth's climate and the survival of many species.

The Atmosphere

The mixture of gases that make up the atmosphere are most commonly referred to as air. The main gases that make up the atmosphere are nitrogen and oxygen. About 78% of the atmosphere is nitrogen. Oxygen makes up about 21% of the atmosphere. The remaining 1% is made up of other gases including argon and carbon dioxide. The atmosphere has many functions, including protecting people from the sun's damaging rays and helping to maintain the right temperature for life on Earth.

Every day you are aware of how the atmosphere affects Earth by weather. Weather refers to atmospheric conditions at a particular time and place. Climate differs from weather, because climate is the average pattern of weather that occurs in a certain location over many years. Weather changes quickly due to the constant movement of Earth's atmosphere. Changes to climate take place slowly over a very long time period.

Atmospheric factors that affect weather on a global scale include wind systems and areas of high and low pressure. The jet stream is a wind system of strong air currents that mostly flow from west to east. Air moves from areas of cool, high pressure to areas of warm, low pressure. A cold, high-pressure air mass can bring cool, dry weather. A warm, low-pressure air mass can bring thunderstorms, wind, and precipitation.

Interactions between the atmosphere and the hydrosphere also impact weather patterns. Ocean currents and water temperature are important to the formation of weather systems, such as tropical storms and hurricanes. Warm, ocean water can evaporate into the atmosphere and then condense and release energy that drives tropical storms. Ocean water contains stream-like movements of water called ocean currents. The Gulf Stream is an ocean current that transports warm water. It flows up the east coast of North America, then toward Europe. This current keeps temperatures mild in Florida and in Europe's British Isles.

Layers of the Atmosphere

Earth's atmosphere is divided into four layers based on temperature and other properties. Its layers are the troposphere, the stratosphere, the mesosphere, and the thermosphere. The troposphere is the lowest layer of the atmosphere. It is closest to Earth and contains the air we breathe. Half of the matter in our atmosphere is found in the troposphere, and most weather that we experience, such as clouds and storms, happens here, too.

The stratosphere is the layer above the troposphere. Airplanes are flown in this part of the atmosphere because there are fewer disturbances there, making the air more stable. The ozone layer in the stratosphere absorbs ultraviolet radiation from the sun, which warms the air. Gases in the stratosphere are layered and do not mix very much.

The mesosphere sits on top of the stratosphere. In this layer, the temperature decreases as the altitude increases. If you have ever seen a shooting star, you have observed an event in the mesosphere. When meteors hit Earth's atmosphere, the mesosphere is the layer in which they burn up.

The thermosphere is the uppermost layer of the atmosphere. The temperature increases as the altitude increases because gases absorb high-energy solar radiation. This layer of the atmosphere can reach temperatures of 2000°C (3632°F)!

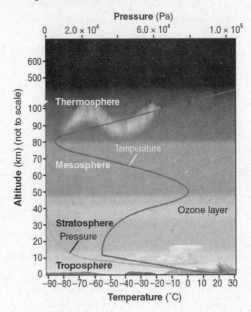

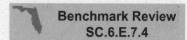

The Biosphere

The biosphere is made up of living things and the areas of Earth where they are found. The rocks, soil, oceans, lakes, rivers, and lower atmosphere all support life. Organisms have even been found deep in Earth's crust and high in clouds. No matter where they live, all organisms need certain factors to survive. Many organisms need oxygen or carbon dioxide to carry out life processes. Liquid water is also important for most living things. Many organisms also need moderate temperatures.

You will not find a polar bear living in a desert because it is too hot for the polar bear. However, some organisms do live in extreme environments, such as in ice at the poles and at volcanic vents on the sea floor. A stable source of energy is also important for life. For example, plants and algae use the energy from sunlight to make their food. Other organisms get their energy by eating these plants or algae.

Student-Response Activity

1 How does the biosphere rely on the other spheres for survival?

_____

_____

_____

_____

2 Think about the layers of the atmosphere. What are two ways that the atmosphere helps protect life on Earth?

_____

_____

3 How does the movement of warm air masses affect local weather?

_____

_____

4 Use this image to give two examples of how the water cycle affects different Earth spheres.

_____

_____

_____

_____

Benchmark Assessment SC.6.E.7.4

Fill in the letter of the best choice.

1 Marla is building a model to show the location of all water on Earth. Which two spheres contain **most** of Earth's water?

(A) hydrosphere and cryosphere

(B) hydrosphere and geosphere

(C) geosphere and cryosphere

(D) cryosphere and biosphere

2 Examine the image shown below.

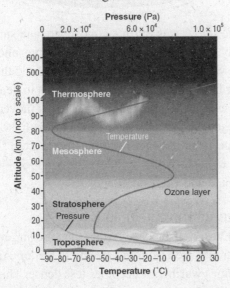

In which layer of the atmosphere does weather occur?

(F) Mesosphere

(G) Stratosphere

(H) Thermosphere

(I) Troposphere

3 How can ocean currents affect local weather?

(A) Ocean currents can cause cloud formation.

(B) Ocean currents can cause heavy winds and high waves.

(C) Ocean currents can transport clouds from place to place.

(D) Ocean currents can affect air temperature.

4 Which sentence describes a location's climate?

(F) Current conditions could lead to a tornado.

(G) Rain is in the forecast for tomorrow evening.

(H) Over the past 20 years, the average summer is 24°C (76°F).

(I) The high this weekend is expected to be 21°C (70°F).

5 What does warm water carried by the Gulf Stream to the North Atlantic Ocean cause?

(A) a harsh winter in Florida

(B) a cold-water surface current that flows to the coast of Florida

(C) a warm-water surface current that flows along the coast of California

(D) a mild climate for the coast of Florida

Name _____ Date _____

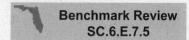
SC.6.E.7.5 Explain how energy provided by the sun influences global patterns of atmospheric movement and the temperature differences between air, water, and land.

How Energy from the Sun Influences Earth

Radiation

Like other stars, the sun is a gigantic nuclear furnace. By combining, or fusing, atoms together, the sun releases massive amounts of energy. The sun transfers energy to Earth by radiation. **Radiation** is the transfer of energy as electromagnetic waves. Radiation can transfer energy between objects that are not in direct contact with each other. Energy from the sun is called **electromagnetic radiation.** This energy is essential to nearly all life on Earth, and is a major source of energy for processes at Earth's surface.

Energy Moves from Land to Air

Like the ocean and the atmosphere, the sun also heats land. Radiation from the sun hits land and transfers energy, causing the ground to warm. Water and air can move freely, but land cannot. Even so, thermal energy stored in the ground can also be transferred. Some energy is released from the ground as radiation. Have you ever felt heat rising from the ground after a sunny day? If so, you have felt radiation. Thermal energy in the ground can also be transferred by conduction. When your feet get too hot from walking on sand or pavement, you are experiencing conduction. Both conduction and radiation can transfer thermal energy from the ground to the atmosphere. In this way, energy that enters Earth's system at any place can affect any other place on Earth.

Convection

When thermal energy is transferred by the movement of particles, it is called convection. Have you ever watched a pot of boiling water? If so, you have seen convection. **Convection** is the transfer of energy due to the movement of matter. As water warms up at the bottom of the pot, some of the hot water rises. At the same time, cooler water from other parts of the pot sink and replace the rising water. This water is then warmed, and the cycle continues.

The sun warms Earth's atmosphere and surface unevenly. As areas in the ocean or the atmosphere become warmer, the particles spread out, and the air or water becomes less dense. Differences in density can cause movement in air or water. This movement also causes thermal energy to move through the substance. Thermal energy is transferred from warmer to colder areas by convection in the atmosphere and oceans.

Patterns of Movement on Earth

If Earth's surface is warmer than the air, energy will be transferred from the ground to the air. As the air becomes warmer, it becomes less dense. This air is pushed upward and out of the way by cooler, denser air that is sinking. As the warm air rises, it cools, becomes denser and begins to sink back toward Earth's surface. This cycle of warm air rising and cool air sinking is called a **convection current**.

Air moves from areas of high pressure to areas of low pressure. This movement of air is what we call wind. The greater the pressure difference, the faster the wind moves. Certain wind patterns are very reliable and predictable. The polar jet stream is one example of a wind pattern. The polar jet stream is a stream of wind that blows from west to east in the northern hemisphere. This wind pattern is partly caused by the difference in temperature between the polar region and the temperate region at lower latitudes. Because warm air is less dense and has lower pressure, the higher-pressure, colder air from the polar region moves south. The rotation of Earth causes the wind to blow from west to east. The result of this wind pattern is that weather systems tend to move from west to east in the United States.

Convection currents also occur in the ocean because of differences in the density of ocean water. More dense water sinks to the ocean floor, and less dense water moves toward the surface.

The density of ocean water is influenced by temperature and the amount of salt in the water. Cold water is denser than warmer water. Water that contains a lot of salt is more dense than less-salty water.

Energy produced deep inside Earth heats rock in the mantle. The heated rock becomes less dense and is pushed up toward Earth's surface by the cooler, denser surrounding rock. Once cooled near the surface, the rock sinks. These convection currents transfer energy from Earth's core toward Earth's surface. These currents also cause the movement of tectonic plates.

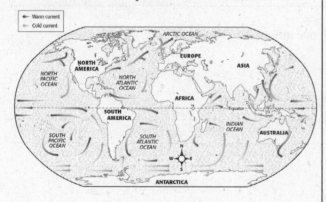

Conduction

Have you ever touched an ice cube and wondered why it feels cold? An ice cube has only a small amount of energy, compared to your hand. Energy is transferred to the ice cube from your hand through the process of conduction. **Conduction** is the transfer of energy from one object to another object through direct contact. Thermal energy can also be transferred directly from particle to particle. Even a solid block of ice has particles in constant motion. Conduction involves the faster-moving particles of the warmer object transferring energy to the slower-moving particles in the cooler object. The greater the difference in energy of the particles, the faster the transfer of energy by conduction occurs.

Conduction allows thermal energy to move between land, the atmosphere, and the ocean. Interactions between the ocean and the atmosphere drive global weather patterns. Energy can be transferred between the geosphere and the atmosphere by conduction. When cooler air molecules come into direct contact with the warm ground, energy is passed to the air by conduction. Conduction between the ground and the air happens only within a few centimeters of Earth's surface.

Conduction also happens between particles of air and particles of water. For example, if air transfers enough energy to liquid water, the water may evaporate. If water vapor transfers energy to the air, the kinetic energy of the water decreases. As a result, the water vapor may condense to form liquid water droplets. Inside Earth, energy transfers between rock particles by conduction. However, rock is a poor conductor of heat, so this process happens very slowly.

Student-Response Activity

1 How does each process contribute to the circulation of the atmosphere?

- Convection

  _____

  _____

- Conduction

  _____

  _____

- Radiation

  _____

  _____

2 Is the following statement true or false? Explain your answer.

"Energy from the sun tends to affect only a small part of Earth's system."

_____

_____

3 Read each statement. Identify the process in each one as *conduction, convection,* or *radiation.* Explain your answer.

- Julio cooks an egg in a hot pan.

  _____

  _____

- Eva sits in front of a fire to keep warm.

  _____

  _____

- Water boils in a pot.

  _____

  _____

4 Provide an example of how energy from the sun affects patterns of movement in the ocean.

_____

_____

_____

Benchmark Assessment SC.6.E.7.5

Fill in the letter of the best choice.

1 Jasmine is riding in a hot air balloon. She wants to know how the balloon is able to lift her into the atmosphere. Which **best** explains how the hot air balloon works?

(A) The balloon rises because conduction of thermal energy always happens in an upward direction.

(B) The balloon rises because conduction of thermal energy pushes against the inside of the balloon.

(C) The balloon rises because convection causes the warmer air inside the balloon to rise in the cool atmosphere.

(D) The balloon rises because radiation from the sun causes the atmosphere around the balloon to be less dense.

2 Jermaine described how he saw steam rise from a puddle after the sun came out. Which processes did he observe?

(F) conduction and radiation

(G) convection and conduction

(H) radiation and convection

(I) convection, conduction, and radiation

3 One morning before the sun rose, Cole noticed it was very warm outside. Later that day, Cole noticed it became colder. Which statement **best** explains why it became colder as the day went on?

(A) Warm air tends to move away from an area quickly.

(B) Cold air tends to sink in the atmosphere throughout the day.

(C) Radiation from the sun strikes Earth most directly early in the day.

(D) Energy from the sun causes the atmosphere to move continuously.

4 There is a convection current present in part of an ocean. Which statement describes the **most likely** result of the convection current?

(F) The water in that area will swirl horizontally.

(G) The water at the surface will sink, and deeper water will rise.

(H) The water will cool rapidly as heat dissipates in all directions.

(I) The water beneath the surface will move towards polar regions.

5 People harness the sun's energy in many ways. Which is **not** a result of the sun's energy?

(A) Energy is generated by turbines moved by wind.

(B) Energy is generated by capturing heat from underground.

(C) Energy is generated by using ocean currents to turn turbines.

(D) Energy is generated by capturing radiant energy collected by mirrors.

SC.8.P.8.4 Classify and compare substances on the basis of characteristic physical properties that can be demonstrated or measured; for example, density, thermal or electrical conductivity, solubility, magnetic properties, melting and boiling points, and know that these properties are independent of the amount of the sample.

Classifying Substances Using Physical Properties

Common Physical Properties

Normally, when describing an object, you identify what it is about that object that you can observe without changing its identity. A **physical property** is a characteristic of a substance that can be observed without changing the identity of the substance. The physical properties of a substance often describe how the substance can be useful. Some common physical properties are density, thermal conductivity, electrical conductivity, solubility, magnetic attraction, and melting and boiling point.

Density

Which would you rather have fall on your foot—a brick or a foam block that is the size of the brick? Even though both are the same size, the mass of the brick is much greater than the mass of the foam block! You can identify each block by its density. **Density** is a measure of the amount of matter in a given amount of volume. For example, 1.0 g of liquid water has a volume of 1.0 mL, liquid water has a density of 1.0 g/mL.

Densities of Common Substances*			
Substance	**Density (g/cm^3)**	**Substance**	**Density (g/cm^3)**
Water (liquid)	1.00	Silver (solid)	10.50
Iron pyrite (solid)	5.02	Lead (solid)	11.35
Zinc (solid)	7.13	Mercury (liquid)	13.55
Copper (solid)	8.96	Gold (solid)	19.32

*at 20ºC and normal atmospheric pressure

To find an object's density (D), first measure its mass (m) and volume (V). Then, use the equation below.

$$density = mass/volume$$

Units for density consist of a mass unit divided by a volume unit. The density units most often used are grams per cubic centimeter (g/cm^3) for solids and grams per milliliter (g/mL) for liquids. The density of a given substance remains the same no matter how much of the substance you have. That is, the density of 1 cm^3 of a substance is equal to the density of 1 km^3 of that substance.

Thermal Conductivity and Electrical Conductivity

Have you ever put a metal spoon in a hot beverage? The end of the spoon gets warm very quickly. This is an example of **conduction**, or the transmission of heat or electricity through a medium. Thermal conductivity is the rate at which a substance transfers heat. Electrical conductivity is a measure of how well an electric current can move through a substance.

Solubility

When you mix sugar and water, you are making a **solution**. The **solute** is the substance that dissolves and the **solvent** is the substance that does the dissolving. Many solutions are water based. That is, the solvent is water. **Solubility** is the ability of a substance to dissolve in another substance. There is a limit to how much sugar you can dissolve in a given amount of water at a particular temperature. A solvent into which no more solute can be dissolved is said to have reached **saturation**.

The table below shows the solubility of a few common substances in 100 mL of water at 20 °C.

Solute	Grams of solute dissolved in 100 mL of water at 20°C
baking soda	10
table salt	38
table sugar	205

Temperature also affects the solubility of a substance. For most solids, as temperature increases, solubility increases. That is why more sugar can dissolve in hot tea than iced tea! When the solute is a gas like carbon dioxide (CO_2), as the temperature increases, the solubility decreases. That is why warm soda goes flat faster than cold soda; the fizz (bubbles of carbon dioxide) do not remain dissolved and rise to the surface of the liquid.

Magnetic Attraction

Have you ever used a magnet to pick up a string of metal paper clips? Some substances like iron, cobalt, nickel, and steel are attracted to magnets, while others are not. Magnetic attraction can act at a distance. It takes place because the electrons in certain substances line up in a special way.

Melting Point and Boiling Point

One easily observed physical property is the state of matter, which is the physical form in which a substance exists. Solids, liquids, and gases are three common states of matter. The **melting point** of a substance is the temperature at which it can change from a solid to a liquid. The **boiling point** of a substance is the temperature at which a liquid changes to a gas. Regardless of what state a substance is in, it is always that substance. For example, water is always water whether it is a solid, liquid, or gas.

Identifying Substances

The physical properties of conductivity, solubility, magnetism, melting point, and boiling point are **intrinsic** properties. This means that they are the result of the substance itself, and not caused by anything outside of the substance. Scientists can use known intrinsic properties to identify unknown substances. It does not matter how large or small of a sample the scientist may have. Intrinsic properties remain the same independent of the size of the sample. The density of pure water, for example, is 1 g/mL. Regardless of whether you test a liter or a fraction of a milliliter of water, the density will always be 1 g/mL.

Student-Response Activity

1 What is the density, in grams per milliliter (g/mL), of a substance with a mass of 50 grams and a volume of 100 mL? Explain your answer.

_____

_____

_____

_____

_____

Isaiah has samples of two different elements, one metal and one nonmetal. Some properties of the samples are shown in the table below. Use the table to answer Questions 2–3.

Property	Sample A	Sample B
Melting point (°C)	1083	217
Conducts heat	yes	no

② What can Isaiah conclude about the identity of Sample A?

_____

_____

_____

③ What can Isaiah conclude about the identity of Sample B?

_____

_____

④ Emma is working in the laboratory to determine the density of a rectangular piece of solid iron. What are two tools Emma should use to determine the density of the iron?

_____

_____

_____

⑤ Does observing a physical property of a substance change the identity of the substance? Explain your answer.

_____

_____

_____

⑥ James dissolves 20 g of table salt in 100 mL of water at 20°C. What prediction can you make about what will happen if all 100 mL of water are boiled away?

_____

_____

_____

Benchmark Assessment SC.8.P.8.4

Fill in the letter of the best choice.

❶ Which is **true** about density?

(A) A possible unit for density is grams.

(B) Liquid gold is denser than solid gold.

(C) Density is found by multiplying mass and volume.

(D) Density is independent of the amount of the sample.

❷ Examine the image shown below.

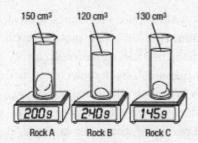

150 cm³   120 cm³   130 cm³

200g   240g   145g

Rock A   Rock B   Rock C

A student measured the volume of three rocks. The diagram above shows the results of her investigation. Which correctly orders the rocks from least to greatest?

(F) Rock A, Rock B, Rock C

(G) Rock C, Rock A, Rock B

(H) Rock B, Rock C, Rock A

(I) Rock A, Rock C, Rock B

❸ What is the melting point of a substance?

(A) When its temperature changes from a gas to a liquid.

(B) When its temperature changes from a liquid to a solid.

(C) When its temperature changes from a liquid to a gas.

(D) When its temperature changes from a solid to a liquid.

❹ Which physical property is the rate at which a substance transfers heat?

(F) boiling point

(G) density

(H) electrical conductivity

(I) thermal conductivity

❺ Lisa is using a magnet to pick up various objects. Which object is **not** attracted to her magnet?

(A) cobalt

(B) iron

(C) nickel

(D) wood

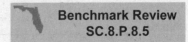
SC.8.P.8.5 Recognize that there are a finite number of elements and that their atoms combine in a multitude of ways to produce compounds that make up all of the living and nonliving things that we encounter.

Scientific Theory of Atoms

What is in an Atom?

Matter is made of particles, which we call atoms. An **atom** is the smallest unit of an element that maintains the properties of that element. Almost all atoms are made of the same three particles. These particles are protons, neutrons, and electrons.

Protons are positively charged particles found within the nucleus. **Neutrons** are the particles of the nucleus that have no electric charge. **Electrons** are the negatively charged particles in atoms. Electrons are found outside the nucleus in electron clouds.

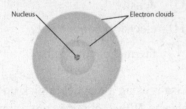

Nucleus   Electron clouds

Atoms can be combined in different ways to produce different substances. The substances you encounter every day can be classified into one of three classes of matter—elements, compounds, and mixtures.

Atoms are the building blocks of matter. Atoms make up elements and compounds. An **element** is made up of one or more of the same kind of atom chemically combined. The atomic number of an element is the number of protons in the nucleus of an atom of that element. All atoms of a given element have the same number of protons in the nucleus. Atoms with different atomic numbers are atoms of different elements.

A **compound** is made up of different kinds of atoms chemically combined. Compounds have different properties from the elements that make them up. Elements and compounds, in turn, make up mixtures. A **mixture** contains a variety of elements and compounds that are not chemically combined with each other.

Pure Substances

Elements and compounds are pure substances. A **pure substance** is a substance that has definite physical and chemical properties such as appearance, melting point, and reactivity. No matter the amount of a pure substance you have, it will always have the same properties. This is because pure substances are made up of one type of particle.

Compounds are also pure substances, such as water. Two different kinds of atoms make up each chemically combined particle, or *molecule*. Every water molecule is identical. Each molecule is made up of exactly two hydrogen atoms and one oxygen atom. Because water is a pure substance, we can define certain properties of water. For example, at standard pressure, water always freezes at 0 °C and boils at 100 °C.

Physical changes such as melting, freezing, cutting, or smashing do not change the identity of pure substances. For example, if you cut copper pipe into short pieces, the material is still copper. And if you freeze liquid water, the particles that make up the ice remain the same— two hydrogen atoms combined with one oxygen atom.

Classifying Elements

Differences in physical and chemical properties allow us to classify elements. By knowing the category to which an element belongs, you can predict some of its properties. Elements are broadly classified as metals, nonmetals, or metalloids. Most metals are shiny, conduct heat and electricity well, and can be shaped into thin sheets and wires. Nonmetals are not shiny and do not conduct heat or electricity well. Metalloids have some properties of both metals and nonmetals.

The Periodic Table

There are over 100 elements known to exist. Each element has a place in an arrangement called the periodic table of the elements. The periodic table is a useful tool that can help you to identify elements that have similar properties.

Each vertical column of elements (from top to bottom) on the periodic table is called a group. Elements in the same group often have similar physical and chemical properties.

Dmitri Mendeleev, a Russian chemist, made a scientific contribution by discovering a pattern to the elements in 1869. Mendeleev saw that when the elements were arranged in order of increasing atomic mass, those that had similar properties fell into a repeating pattern. That is, the pattern was periodic. **Periodic** means happening at regular intervals. In the early 1900s, the scientist Henry Moseley rearranged Mendeleev's periodic table in order of increasing number of protons (increasing atomic number). These are the numbers above the element symbols in the table below.

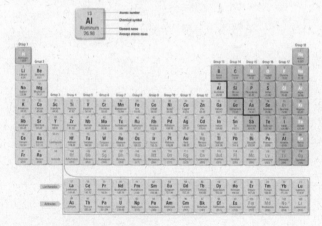

Classifying Compounds

There are many ways to classify compounds. Many compounds are acids or bases. In the following table, vinegar is an acid, and ammonia is a base. Acids and bases have special properties that help us identify them. Scientists use a numerical scale that measures how acidic or basic a substance is. This is called the pH scale. Acids taste sour, react with many metals, and have a low pH number. All acids contain at least one hydrogen (H) atom. Acids can be found in things such as lemons and car batteries.

Familiar Compounds	
Compound	**Elements Combined**
Table salt (NaCl)	sodium(Na) and chlorine(Cl)
Water (H_2O)	hydrogen(H) and oxygen(O)
Vinegar ($C_2H_4O_2$)	hydrogen(H), carbon(C), and oxygen(O)
Ammonia (NH_3)	nitrogen(N) and hydrogen (H)

Bases taste bitter, feel slippery, and have a high pH. Some examples include soap and drain cleaners. Bases accept hydrogen atoms from acids. When an acid and a base are combined, a chemical reaction will occur. If an acid and base of equal strength are combined in equal amounts, then the solution will **neutralize**. That means the solution will be neither acidic nor basic, and will have a pH of 7.

Sometimes, a neutralization reaction will form a salt. Salts are neutral substances formed from two oppositely charged (one positive and one negative) groups. When dissolved in water, the positive and negative ions that form a salt will separate. Elements and compounds are all pure substances. That means that they are made of only one kind of molecule.

Mixtures

A **mixture** is a combination of elements or compounds that are not chemically combined. In other words, mixtures contain more than one type of substance. Mixtures do not have a specific ratio of elements, so they are not pure substances.

Familiar Mixtures	
Mixture	**Substances Combined**
Air	Nitrogen (N_2) and oxygen (O_2)
Milk	Water (H_2O) lactose
Lemonade	Water (H_2O) sucrose

It is clear that something is a mixture when you can see the different substances in it. For example, if you scoop up a handful of soil, it might contain dirt, rocks, leaves, and even insects. Exactly what you see depends on what part of the soil is scooped. Mixtures can be classified as suspensions, solutions, or colloids.

Name _____ Date _____

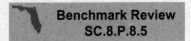
Suspensions are mixtures in which the particles of a material are spread throughout a liquid or gas, but are too large to stay mixed without being stirred or shaken. If a suspension is allowed to sit, the particles will settle out. A snow globe is an example of a suspension.

In a **solution**, one substance is dissolved in another substance. When you make tea, some of the compounds inside the tea leaves dissolve in the hot water. These compounds give your tea its unique color and taste. Many familiar solutions are liquids. However, solutions may also be gases or solids. Air is an example of a gaseous solution. Alloys, such as brass and steel, are solid solutions in which substances are dissolved in metals.

Colloids are a third type of mixture that falls somewhere between suspensions and solutions. As in a suspension, the particles in a colloid are spread throughout a liquid or gas. Unlike the particles in a suspension, colloid particles are small and do not settle out quickly. Milk and gelatin are colloids.

How is Matter Arranged?

As you know, all matter is made of atoms or groups of atoms. These atoms are in constant motion. How much the particles move and how often they bump into each other determine the state of matter of the substance.

All types of matter can exist in three phases: solids, liquids, and gases. In the solid state, particles are close together and only vibrate in place. In liquids, the particles have more energy and can move around. On average, particles in a liquid are farther apart from one another than they would be in a solid form. In gases, the particles have lots of energy, so they can move fast and far away from one another.

Student-Response Activity

1 Wendy wants to find out if a substance is an acid or a base. What are two ways that Wendy could investigate to find out what kind of substance it is?

_____

_____

_____

_____

2 Identify the three subatomic particles. Where are each of the particles located within the atom?

_____

_____

_____

_____

_____

Name ______________________ Date __________

Benchmark Review
SC.8.P.8.5

3 How does saltwater differ in its composition from distilled water?

4 What do elements in the same column of the periodic table have in common?

5 How can the motion of atoms in the solid state of most substances be described?

Benchmark Assessment SC.8.P.8.5

Fill in the letter of the best choice.

1 Which **best** describes how to classify water?

Ⓐ It is an element because it is made from a pure substance.

Ⓑ It is a compound because it is made of a single kind of molecule.

Ⓒ It is a mixture because it is composed of more than one molecule.

Ⓓ It is a solution because it is a homogenous mixture of different compounds.

2 Which **best** describes an acid?

Ⓕ a soapy substance that is nonreactive with metals

Ⓖ a neutral substance made of oppositely charged particles

Ⓗ a caustic substance that has a high number on the pH scale

Ⓘ a sour liquid that forms gas bubbles when mixed with copper

3 Which is **not** a property of an acid?

Ⓐ tastes sour

Ⓑ has a high pH

Ⓒ reacts with metals

Ⓓ contains the element hydrogen

4 Magnesium (Mg), Calcium (Ca), and Barium (Ba) are all in the same group on the periodic table. What do these elements have in common?

Ⓕ They all have the same atomic number.

Ⓖ They all have the same number of electrons.

Ⓗ They all react with substances in similar ways.

Ⓘ They were all discovered by Dmitri Mendeleev.

5 Tyson draws a model to show how the particles in a liquid appear. Which model (or models) could represent this?

1   2   3

Ⓐ Model 1

Ⓑ Model 3

Ⓒ Model 1 and Model 2

Ⓓ Model 1, Model 2, and Model 3

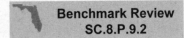
SC.8.P.9.2 Differentiate between physical changes and chemical changes.

Physical and Chemical Changes

Physical Changes

A physical property of matter is any property that can be observed or measured without changing the chemical identity of the substance. A **physical change** is a change that affects one or more physical properties of a substance. For example, the appearance, shape, or size of a substance may be altered during a physical change. Physical changes occur when a substance changes from one form to another. However, the chemical identity of the substance remains the same.

For example, physical changes can be used to separate the mixture of the solids sulfur and sodium chloride (table salt). Water is added to the mixture. The salt dissolves in water, while the sulfur floats on top. During the separation process, the form of each substance changed, but the identity of each substance did not. Liquid water freezing into ice is another example of a physical change. Most physical changes are reversible, because physical changes affect only the form. They do not affect the identity of the matter.

Chemical Changes

Elements combine by reacting with one another. A **chemical change**, or reaction, happens when one or more substances change into new substances that have entirely different properties. Chemical changes happen when bonds between atoms are broken, or new bonds are formed to make new substances. A chemical equation shows what happens during a chemical reaction to produce new substances. For example, look closely at the following equation:

$$2KI + Pb(NO_3)_2 \rightarrow PbI_2 + 2KNO_3$$

Notice that the elements K and Pb have "switched places." The right side of this equation shows the new substances that are formed. You can see that their chemical formulas are different from those of the substances on the left side of the

equation. So, a chemical reaction involves the rearrangement of atoms to produce substances that have new properties.

Chemical changes occur frequently in nature. One of the most important chemical changes in nature happens when green plants make food. In this process, called **photosynthesis**, plants use energy from sunlight to change water and carbon dioxide into oxygen and molecules of glucose. In animals, chemical changes occur during digestion.

Digestion is the process of breaking down food, such as a peanut butter and jelly sandwich, into a form that can pass from the digestive tract into the bloodstream. There are two types of digestion— mechanical and chemical. The breaking, crushing, and mashing of food is called mechanical digestion. These processes are examples of physical changes. In chemical digestion, large molecules are broken down into nutrients. Nutrients are substances in food that the body needs for normal growth, maintenance, and repair.

Evidence of Chemical Change

There are clues you can look for in the laboratory that indicate a chemical change may have occurred. A change in color or the production of heat, sound, or light are some of these clues. For example, fizzing and foaming signal that a chemical change happens when vinegar and baking soda are mixed. New substances, including carbon dioxide gas, form. Another example is the burning of wood, which has the chemical property of flammability. As wood and oxygen react, they change into new substances having different properties from the original wood and oxygen. Unlike physical changes, most chemical changes are not reversible.

Evidence of Chemical Changes
absorption or release of energy, usually as heat
formation of a gas
formation of a solid (precipitate)
change in color

Energy in Chemical Changes

Temperature influences chemical changes. Endothermic reactions are those that absorb energy. If there is little energy available in the environment, then the chemical reaction will occur slowly or not at all. Photosynthesis in plants is an example of an endothermic reaction. Light energy from the sun drives the formation of glucose from carbon dioxide and water. Exothermic reactions are those in which energy is given off. For example, when a candle burns, carbon dioxide, water, and heat are produced.

The Law of Conservation of Mass

The **law of conservation of mass** states that in ordinary chemical and physical changes, mass is not created or destroyed, but is only transformed into different substances. When physical and chemical changes take place, atoms mix and rearrange. However, the total mass of the components does not change. For example, when sugar and water are mixed, the mass of the solution equals the sum of the masses of the sugar and the water. Even though the components are mixed, mass is conserved. Look at this equation again:

$$2KI + Pb(NO_3)_2 \rightarrow PbI_2 + 2KNO_3$$

You can see that even though the K and Pb atoms switch places, the number of each atom is the same on both sides of the equation. Mass is neither created nor destroyed in chemical or physical changes. For example, suppose you have a glass of ice water. The water may freeze, or the ice may melt, but the amount of matter (water) in the glass will stay the same.

Student-Response Activity

❶ Amanda dissolves some sugar in water in a beaker. She allows the water to evaporate and notices that solid sugar remains in the bottom of the beaker. What two pieces of evidence can be provided to show that this is a physical change?

_____

_____

_____

_____

❷ Two colorless solutions are mixed together in a test tube. A student observes that a bright yellow solid collects at the bottom of the test tube. Is this is physical or chemical change? Cite evidence to support your answer.

_____

_____

_____

_____

3 Complete the Venn diagram to compare and contrast physical and chemical changes.

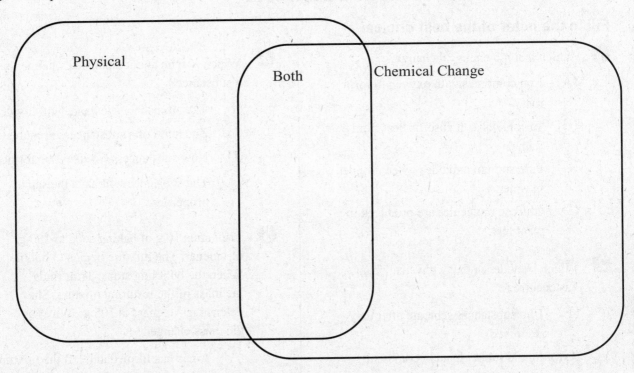

Physical   Both   Chemical Change

4 A student observes the chemical process described by this equation:

$4Al + 3O_2 \rightarrow 2Al_2O_3$

How does the mass of the new substance compare to the total mass of the starting materials?

_____
_____
_____
_____
_____

5 Suppose a log's mass is 5 kg. After burning, the mass of the ash is 1 kg. What would you infer has happened to the other 4 kg?

_____
_____
_____
_____
_____

Benchmark Assessment SC.8.P.9.2

Fill in the letter of the best choice.

1 Which is **not** a chemical change?

(A) Iron combines with oxygen to form rust.

(B) Wax melts as it absorbs heat from a flame.

(C) Pure sodium explodes when dropped in water.

(D) Glucose molecules are produced in a plant leaf.

2 Which is evidence that a physical change has occurred?

(F) Two substances separate after they are mixed.

(G) An old rubber band becomes stiff and brittle.

(H) A blue powder-like substance forms on a battery.

(I) A sealed bag filled with powder and water expands.

3 A student dissolves 5 g of table salt in 100 mL of water in a beaker. Compared to the total mass of the salt and water before mixing, which is **true**?

(A) The total mass of the solution will increase by a small amount.

(B) The total mass of the solution will increase by a large amount.

(C) The total mass of the solution will decrease by a small amount.

(D) The total mass of the solution will neither increase nor decrease.

4 Which is **true** about a physical change to a substance?

(F) The atoms in a substance will divide.

(G) The mass of a substance will increase.

(H) New substances will likely be formed.

(I) The substance will have the same properties.

5 Trini adds 10 g of baking soda to 100 g of vinegar. The mixture begins to bubble. When the bubbling stops, Trini finds the mass of the resulting mixture. She determines its mass is 105 g. Why has the mass changed?

(A) A gas has formed and left the mixture.

(B) Vinegar evaporated during the experiment.

(C) Mixtures are always less massive than their parts.

(D) Matter was destroyed when vinegar reacted with baking soda.

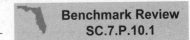

SC.7.P.10.1 Illustrate that the sun's energy arrives as radiation with a wide range of wavelengths, including infrared, visible, and ultraviolet, and that white light is made up of a spectrum of many different colors.

Radiation and Light

Radiation from the Sun

Light is a type of energy that travels as a wave, but light is different from other types of waves. Light waves are vibrating electric and magnetic fields moving through space that transfer energy. When an electrically charged particle vibrates, its fields also vibrate, producing an electromagnetic (EM) wave. This vibration carries energy released by the original vibration of the particle. **Radiation** is energy that has been transmitted by waves or particles, so this transfer of energy is called EM radiation.

Most electromagnetic waves Earth receives from the sun are infrared light, ultraviolet light, and visible light. When you are out in the sun and you feel warm, you feel infrared light from the sun as heat. You might wear sunglasses outside to protect your eyes from ultraviolet light. Too much exposure to ultraviolet light can damage cells.

The Color of Light

Light comes in many colors, from red to violet. Like all waves, light has wavelengths. Different wavelengths of light are interpreted by our eyes as different colors. The shortest wavelengths are seen as violet, and the longest ones are seen as red. Even the longest wavelengths we can see are still very small—less than one ten-thousandth of a centimeter.

White light is what we perceive when we see all the wavelengths of light at once, in equal proportions. A prism can split white light into its component colors, separating the colors by wavelength. The various colors of light can also be recombined to produce white light. Our eyes only register three colors of light, called the primary colors—red, green, and blue. All other colors we see are a mixture of these three colors.

A television or computer screen works by sending signals to make small dots, called pixels, that give off red, green, and blue light.

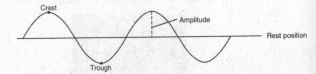

The Electromagnetic Spectrum

EM waves are measured by frequency or by wavelength. The light waves we see are EM waves. However, visible light represents only a very small part of the range of frequencies (or wavelengths) that an EM wave can have. This range is called the **electromagnetic (EM) spectrum**. These other EM waves are the same type of wave as the light we are used to. They are just different frequencies. Two parts of the spectrum are close to visible light. **Infrared**, or IR, light has slightly longer wavelengths than red light. **Ultraviolet**, or UV, light has slightly shorter wavelengths than violet light.

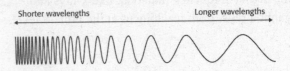

People use forms of light across the electromagnetic spectrum for different functions. Satellites in space can detect electromagnetic radiation from objects and use this to create images. When you listen to the radio, radio waves are transmitting the sound you hear. Radio waves have the longest wavelengths. They are used to broadcast many signals, including radio, television, and alarm systems. Despite their name, microwaves are not the shortest EM waves.

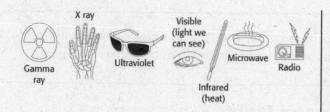

In addition to heating food up quickly, microwaves are used in cellular phones. We feel infrared light as heat. Infrared imaging can locate objects that emit heat by creating a thermogram, which is a visual representation of temperature.

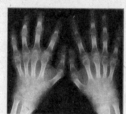

Doctors can use ultraviolet light to sterilize medical equipment, x-rays to make images of a person's bones, and gamma rays to treat some cancers.

Radiation from the Sun

Between the sun and us lies Earth's atmosphere. In order to see anything, some of the sun's light must make it through the atmosphere. However, not all wavelengths of light penetrate the atmosphere equally. The atmosphere blocks most of the higher-frequency radiation, like x-rays and gamma rays, from reaching us at the ground level, while allowing most of the visible light to reach us. There is a "window" of radio frequencies that are barely blocked at all. Radio and visible light penetrate all the way to the ground. Most ultraviolet light is blocked high in the atmosphere.

The atmosphere blocks much of the sun's radiation, but not all. Some EM radiation can be dangerous to humans, so we take extra steps to protect ourselves. Receiving too much ultraviolet (UV) radiation can cause sunburn, skin cancer, or damage to the eyes, so we wear sunscreen and UV-blocking sunglasses to protect us from the UV light that passes through the atmosphere. You need this protection even on overcast days because UV light can travel through clouds.

Outer space is often thought of as being cold, but despite this, one of the biggest dangers to astronauts is from overheating! Outside of Earth's protective atmosphere, the level of dangerous EM radiation is much higher. Also, in the vacuum of space, it is much harder to dispose of any unwanted energy, because there is no surrounding matter (like air) to absorb the extra energy. Astronauts need extra protection from EM radiation in space. This is why astronauts' helmets are made to be highly reflective, using a thin layer of pure gold to reflect back unwanted EM radiation.

Student-Response Activity

1 List, in order, the types of light in the electromagnetic spectrum from largest wavelength to smallest wavelength.

_____

_____

2 Imagine you go outside, and you feel warmth. What causes you to feel warm?

_____

_____

3 Complete the Venn diagram to compare and contrast x-rays and gamma rays.

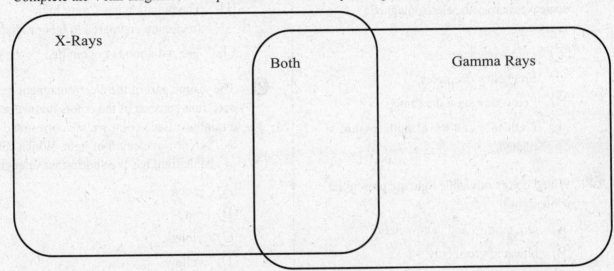

X-Rays   Both   Gamma Rays

4 Suppose you need to heat food. What wave type from the electromagnetic spectrum could you use?

_____

_____

_____

_____

5 What is white light?

_____

_____

_____

_____

Benchmark Assessment SC.7.P.10.1

Fill in the letter of the best choice.

1 Which type of electromagnetic radiation from the sun do you typically perceive on Earth?

(A) gamma rays

(B) infrared waves

(C) radio waves

(D) x-rays

2 What happens to frequency as wavelength decreases across the electromagnetic spectrum?

(F) Frequency increases.

(G) Frequency decreases.

(H) Frequency stays the same.

(I) Frequency and wavelength are not related.

3 Which colors of visible light are present in white light?

(A) red, orange, and yellow only

(B) blue and green only

(C) all colors of light

(D) no colors of light

4 Examine the image shown below.

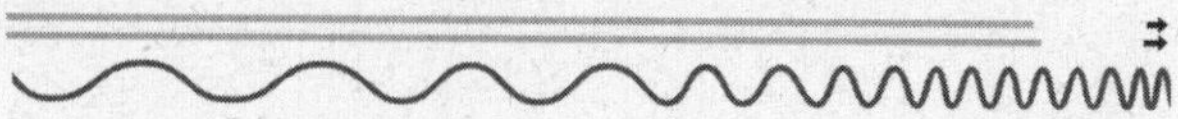

What can you infer about the radiation in the middle of this spectrum?

(F) The radiation is visible.

(G) The radiation can be used to transmit sound.

(H) The radiation has a very high frequency compared to other radiation.

(I) The radiation is not emitted by the sun.

5 The visible part of the electromagnetic spectrum consists of the colors that we see in a rainbow. Each color we see corresponds to a different wavelength of light. Which color of visible light has the shortest wavelength?

(A) green

(B) red

(C) violet

(D) yellow

Name _____ Date _____

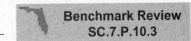
SC.7.P.10.3 Recognize that light waves, sound waves, and other waves move at different speeds in different materials.

Wave Movement

What Are Waves?

The world is full of many types of waves. Sound, light, and water all move in waves. A wave is a disturbance that transfers energy. Waves are caused by the vibration of a **medium**, or the material through which a wave travels. Sound and water waves need a medium to transfer energy. Light waves do not need a medium and can transfer energy from the sun to Earth across empty space.

As a wave moves through a medium, particles may move in different directions or come to rest in different places. The medium may warm up, shift, or change in other ways. Some of the wave's energy produces these changes. As the wave travels through more of the medium, more energy is lost to the medium. Often, higher-frequency waves lose energy more readily than lower-frequency waves. When you stand far from a concert, you might hear only the low-frequency (bass) sounds.

In a **longitudinal wave**, particles move back and forth in the same direction that the wave travels, or parallel to the wave. Sound waves are longitudinal waves. When sound waves pass through the air, particles that make up air move back and forth in the same direction that the sound waves travel.

In a **transverse wave**, particles move up and down, or perpendicularly, to the direction the wave travels. Transverse waves and longitudinal waves often travel at different speeds in a medium. Longitudinal waves are usually faster. For example, an earthquake sends both longitudinal waves (called P-waves) and transverse waves (called S-waves) through Earth's crust. During an earthquake, the faster P-waves arrive first. A little while later the S- waves arrive. The S-waves are slower, but usually more destructive.

A transverse wave and a longitudinal wave can combine to form another kind of wave called a surface wave. Ripples on a pond are an example of a surface wave.

Waves can be classified by the direction of disturbance. They can also be classified by what they are disturbing. Waves that require a medium are called **mechanical waves**. For water waves, water is the medium. For earthquake waves, Earth's crust is the medium.

Some mechanical waves can travel through more than one medium. For example, sound waves can move through air, through water, or even through a solid wall. The waves travel at different speeds in the different media. Sound waves travel much faster in a liquid or a solid than in air. Mechanical waves cannot travel without a medium.

Sunlight travels from the sun to Earth through empty space. Although light waves can travel through a medium, they can also travel without a medium. Light and similar waves are called electromagnetic (EM) waves. **Electromagnetic waves** are disturbances in electric and magnetic fields. They are considered transverse waves. In empty space, all light waves travel at the same speed. This speed, referred to as the speed of light, is about 300 million meters per second!

Amplitude

A wave's **amplitude** is a measure of how far particles in the medium move away from their normal period. For two similar waves, the wave with greater amplitude carries more energy. For example, sound waves with greater amplitude transfer more energy to your eardrum and so they sound louder. As a wave passes, particles in the medium move up and down or back and forth. The points of maximum displacement are called peaks. For a water wave, amplitude is the height of a crest. For other waves, it is the displacement at a peak. You can use a graph of the wave to understand amplitude. The amplitude is half of the difference between the highest and lowest values of the graph. You can use amplitude to describe the height of a wave.

Greater frequency can also mean greater energy in a given amount of time. If waves hit a barrier three times in a minute, they transfer a certain amount of energy to the barrier. If waves of the same amplitude hit nine times in a minute, they transfer more energy in that minute.

Wave Speed

The speed at which a wave travels, wave speed, depends on the properties of the medium. Specifically, wave speed depends on the interactions of the atomic particles of the medium. In general, waves travel faster in solids than in liquids, and faster in liquids than in gases. This is because solids generally have the fastest interactions between particles, and gases have the slowest.

The speed of interactions depends on many factors. For example, wave speed depends on the density of the medium. Waves usually travel slower in the denser of two solids or the denser of two liquids. When the particles are more densely packed, they resist motion more, so they transfer waves more slowly.

In a gas, wave speed depends on temperature as well as density. Particles in hot air move faster than particles in cold air, so particles in hot air collide more often. This faster interaction allows waves to pass through hot air more quickly than through cold air, even though hot air may be less dense. The speed of sound in air at 20 °C is about 340 m/s. The speed of sound in air at 0 °C is slower, about 330 m/s.

Electromagnetic waves do not require a medium, so they can travel in a vacuum. All electromagnetic waves travel at the same speed in empty space. This speed, called the speed of light, is about 300,000,000 m/s. While passing through a medium such as air or glass, EM waves travel more slowly than they do in a vacuum.

Light Waves and Matter

Unlike sound, light can travel through a vacuum that has no matter. Light travels at a constant speed in a vacuum. When light interacts with matter, the matter slows light down. Light travels more slowly through a denser medium. When light strikes an object, the light can be absorbed, reflected, or refracted.

Opaque materials do not let any light pass through them. Instead, they reflect light, absorb light, or both. Many materials, such as wood, brick, or metal, are opaque. When light enters a material but does not leave it, the light is absorbed. **Absorption** is the transfer of light energy to matter.

A book on a table is opaque, because light does not pass through the book, and we cannot see the table beneath. However, absorption is not the only way an object can be opaque.

You see an object only when light from the object enters your eye. However, most objects do not give off, or emit, light. Instead, light bounces off the object's surface. The bouncing of light off a surface is called **reflection**.

Most objects have a surface that is at least slightly rough. When light strikes a rough surface, such as wood or cloth, the light reflects in many different directions. Some of the reflected light reaches your eyes, and you see the object.

Light bounces at an angle equal to the angle at which it hit the surface. When light strikes a smooth or shiny surface such as a mirror, it reflects in a uniform way. As a result, a mirror produces an image. Light from a lamp might be reflected by your skin, then be reflected by a mirror, and then enter your eye. You look at the mirror and see yourself.

Other objects appear to be certain colors because of the wavelength of light that they reflect. For example, grass reflects green light and absorbs other wavelengths, so it appears green. When an object reflects light, the light bounces off of the object.

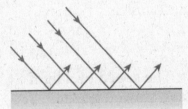

A straight object, such as a straw, looks bent or broken when part of it is underwater. Light from the straw changes direction when it passes from water to glass and from glass to air. **Refraction** is the bending of a wave as it passes from one medium into another at an angle. Your brain always interprets light as traveling in a straight line. You

perceive the straw where it would be if light traveled in a straight line. The light reflected by the straw in air does travel in a straight line to your eye. But the light from the lower part of the straw changes direction when it passes into air. It refracts, causing the illusion that the bottom part of the straw in a water glass is disconnected from the top part.

Refraction is due to the change in speed as a wave enters a new medium. In glass, light's speed depends on wavelength. When light passes through a glass prism, the light waves with shorter wavelengths change direction more than waves with longer wavelengths. So, a prism separates light into a spectrum of colors.

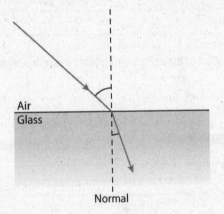

Student-Response Activity

❶ What happens to light in each of the situations below?

absorbed _____

_____

reflected _____

_____

refracted _____

_____

❷ How might an object feel that absorbs light?

_____

_____

❸ Complete the cause-and-effect graphic organizer below.

Cause:_____

_____

_____

_____

_

Effect: The speed of a light
wave slowed down.

❹ What is a mechanical wave? Give an example.

_____

_____

_____

❺ Why does sound travel faster in a solid than in a liquid?

_____

_____

_____

_____

Benchmark Assessment SC.7.P.10.3

Fill in the letter of the best choice.

1 A sound wave travels from air into a swimming pool. How does its speed change?

   (A) It travels faster.

   (B) It travels slower.

   (C) It stops moving.

   (D) It travels at the same speed.

2 Light travels from air into a swimming pool. How does its speed change?

   (F) It travels faster.

   (G) It travels slower.

   (H) It stops moving.

   (I) It travels at the same speed.

3 Examine the image shown below.

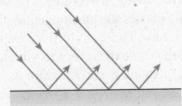

What is happening in this image?

   (A) Light is being absorbed.

   (B) Light is being refracted.

   (C) Light is being reflected.

   (D) Light is traveling through a translucent material.

4 Which happens when sound waves enter a vacuum?

   (F) They are reflected.

   (G) They move slower.

   (H) They move faster.

   (I) They stop moving.

5 Examine the image shown below.

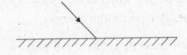

What is happening in this diagram?

   (A) Light is being absorbed.

   (B) Light is being reflected.

   (C) Light is being refracted.

   (D) Light is being transmitted.

SC.7.P.11.2 Investigate and describe the transformation of energy from one form to another.

Energy Transformations

What is Energy?

Energy is the ability to do work or cause change. It is measured in joules (j). Energy exists in many forms. Some of the common forms of energy include mechanical energy, sound energy, electromagnetic energy, chemical energy, thermal energy and heat, and nuclear energy. All forms of energy can be described as one of two types—kinetic energy or potential energy.

Kinetic energy is energy of motion. All moving objects have kinetic energy. The amount of kinetic energy an object has depends on two things—mass and speed. The greater the mass of a moving object, the greater amount of kinetic energy an object has. The faster something moves, the more kinetic energy it has. So a large truck has more kinetic energy than a motorcycle traveling at the same speed because the truck has more mass. Similarly, the kinetic energy of a bowling ball increases as it rolls faster.

Potential energy is the stored energy an object has due to its position or condition. Like kinetic energy, potential energy has the ability to cause change. One type of potential energy is called gravitational potential energy. When you lift an object, you transfer energy to the object and give it gravitational potential energy. The amount of gravitational potential energy an object has depends on its mass and its height above the ground. When you lift your backpack to a chair, you give it gravitational potential energy. If you lift it higher, such as to a table or shelf, you give it a greater amount of gravitational potential energy. If you lift a book to a desk, you give it more gravitational potential energy than when you lift a pencil to the same height because the book weighs more than the pencil.

There are other types of potential energy. Elastic potential energy is related to objects that can stretch or be squeezed, and then regain their strength. This type of energy depends on the characteristics of the object and the distance it is stretched or squeezed. When you pull a bow back to shoot an arrow, you give it elastic potential energy. Stretching a spring or rubber band gives them the same type of energy.

Types of Energy

- **Mechanical energy** is the sum of an object's kinetic energy and potential energy. It is associated with the motion or position of an object. If you lift a book to a shelf, you give it mechanical energy. A bird flying through the sky has mechanical energy.

- **Sound energy** results from the vibrations of particles. When you pluck a guitar string, it vibrates. The vibrating string causes the air molecules around it to vibrate. Those, in turn, cause the air molecules next to them to vibrate. In this way, a sound is carried from its source.

Sound Energy of a Drum

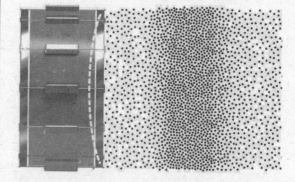

- **Electromagnetic energy** is transmitted through space in the form of electromagnetic waves. Electromagnetic waves can be produced by the vibration of electrically charged particles. Unlike sound, electromagnetic waves can travel through empty space. Light energy is a form of electromagnetic energy. Some examples of electromagnetic energy are visible light, x-rays, and microwaves.

- **Chemical energy** is stored in chemical bonds. If these bonds are broken or rearranged, chemical energy is released or absorbed. Chemical energy is stored in batteries, fuels, and foods.
- **Electrical energy** is the energy of moving electrons. The electrical energy used in your home comes from power plants. Huge generators turn magnets inside loops of wire. The changing position of a magnet makes electrons move in the wire and along the wires from the power plants to electrical stations to your home.
- **Thermal energy** is the energy an object has due to the motion of its molecules. The faster the molecules move, the more thermal energy the object has. Heat is the energy transferred from an object at a higher temperature to an object at a lower temperature.
- **Nuclear energy** comes from the nucleus of an atom. When an atom's nucleus breaks apart, or when the nuclei of two small atoms join together, energy is released. The energy given off by the sun comes from nuclear energy. In the sun, hydrogen nuclei join to make a helium nucleus. This reaction gives off a huge amount of energy. The sun's light and heat come from these reactions. Without nuclear energy from the sun, life would not exist on Earth.

Transformations of Energy

Any form of energy can change into any other form of energy. This change is called an **energy transformation**. Often, one form of energy changes into more than one form.

In many devices, energy undergoes a series of transformations. For example, think about when a person uses gasoline to power a car. In the car engine, chemical energy stored in gasoline is transformed into thermal energy. That thermal energy is used to push part of the engine that makes the car move. So the thermal energy is transformed into mechanical energy.

Kinetic energy can be transformed into potential energy and vice versa. Consider the mass at the end of the spring. In the diagram, the first spring hangs freely so the mass is at the dashed line. When the spring is pulled down, it is given elastic potential energy. When the mass is let go, it moves back up. Because it is moving, it has kinetic energy. The spring squeezes together so the mass is higher than it started. At this point, the mass has elastic potential energy but it also has gravitational potential energy because it lifted the mass higher than it started.

The spring cannot stay like this, so the mass falls back down. As it falls, it is moving again so it has kinetic energy. When it stretches out again, it has elastic potential energy.

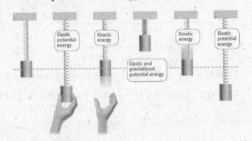

The Law of Conservation of Energy

The **law of conservation of energy** states that energy can be neither created nor destroyed. It can only be transformed. The mechanical energy of an object always remains the same unless some of it is transformed into other forms of energy, such as heat through friction. If no energy is transformed, the mechanical energy of an object stays the same. In order for the mechanical energy to stay the same, some potential energy changes into kinetic energy. At other times, kinetic energy changes into potential energy.

For example, on a roller coaster some mechanical energy gets transformed into sound and thermal energy as it goes down a hill. The total of the coaster's reduced mechanical energy at the bottom of the hill, the increased thermal energy, and the sound energy, is the same amount of energy as the original amount of mechanical energy. In other words, total energy is conserved.

Benchmark Review
SC.7.P.11.2

Student-Response Activity

1 Using your own words, describe the transformation of energy from one form to another. Include an example in your explanation.

_____

_____

2 How do kinetic and potential energy differ?

_____

_____

3 A squirrel carries an acorn to a branch in a tree. The acorn slips off the branch and falls to the ground. Where does the acorn have the **greatest** kinetic energy and the **greatest** potential energy during its fall?

_____

_____

Diedra set up the equipment shown below to study energy transformations. Notice that D shows buzzer. Use the diagram to answer Questions 4–5.

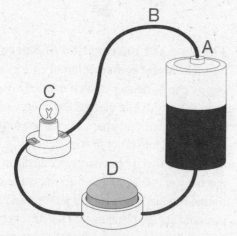

4 Which energy transformation takes place between A and B?

_____

5 Which energy transformation takes place between B and C?

_____

6 How do energy transformations relate to the law of conservation of energy?

_____

_____

Benchmark Assessment SC.7.P.11.2

Fill in the letter of the best choice.

❶ The chart shows some common conversions of energy.

Common Conversions of Electrical Energy	
Alarm clock	electrical energy → light energy and sound energy
Battery	chemical energy → electrical energy
Light bulb	electrical energy → light energy and thermal energy
Blender	electrical energy → kinetic energy and sound energy

Which appliance would you use to convert electrical energy into light energy and sound energy?

Ⓐ alarm clock

Ⓑ battery

Ⓒ blender

Ⓓ light bulb

❷ The chemical energy in a battery is transformed into electrical energy used to power a cell phone. Which statement about this transformation is **true**?

Ⓕ A small amount of energy is destroyed during the transformation.

Ⓖ A large amount of energy is created during the transformation.

Ⓗ The energy is restored to its original form during the transformation.

Ⓘ The total amount of energy remains the same during the transformation.

Look closely at the diagram that shows a roller coaster car at various points along the ride. Use it to answers Questions 3–4.

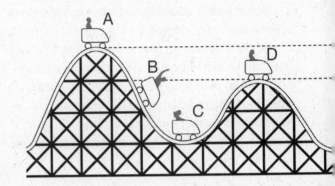

❸ Which energy transformations take place from position A to position D?

Ⓐ potential → kinetic → potential

Ⓑ kinetic → potential → kinetic

Ⓒ potential → kinetic

Ⓓ kinetic → potential

❹ At which position is the roller coaster car's amount of potential energy about equal to the amount of kinetic energy?

Ⓕ Position A

Ⓖ Position B

Ⓗ Position C

Ⓘ Position D

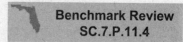
SC.7.P.11.4 Observe and describe that heat flows in predictable ways, moving from warmer objects to cooler ones until they reach the same temperature.

How Does Heat Flow?

Changing and Balancing Temperatures

When heat is added to a substance, the state of the substance may change, making a solid change to a liquid, or a liquid to a gas. When heat is removed, gases can become liquids, and liquids can become solids. When two items of different temperature come into contact with each other, they will eventually reach the same temperature, which will be somewhere between the two initial temperatures. How does this happen?

What is Thermal Energy?

Thermal energy is the total kinetic energy of all particles in a substance and is measured in joules (j). The faster the molecules in an object move, the more thermal energy the object has. Heat always flows from warmer objects to cooler ones. Particles in the warmer object have greater average kinetic energy, so they are moving faster and farther apart. When heat transfers out of the warmer object, its particles slow down, and the temperature decreases. Meanwhile, the heat that is transferred to the cooler object causes its particles to speed up. As a result, the average kinetic energy increases, and the temperature rises. Eventually, the two objects will reach the same temperature. Energy still flows between them, but in both directions so there is no overall change in temperature.

Temperature is a measure of the average kinetic energy of all the particles in an object. In colder liquids, particles are moving slower. In warmer liquids, particles are moving faster. For example, if an iron is hot, the particles in the solid are vibrating very fast and have a high average kinetic energy. If the iron has a low temperature, the particles in the solid are vibrating more slowly and have a lower average kinetic energy.

Heat Can Affect the State of Matter

All matter is made of atoms. These particles are always moving even if they do not appear to be. The **kinetic theory of matter** states that all the particles that make up matter are constantly in motion. The particles that make up matter move around at different speeds. The state of a substance depends on the speed of its particles. The particles in a solid, such as concrete, are not free to move around very much. They vibrate back and forth in the same position and are held tightly together by forces of attraction. The particles in a liquid, such as water in a pool, move much more freely than particles in a solid. They are constantly sliding around and tumbling over each other as they move. In a gas, such as the air around you, particles are far apart and move around at high speeds. Particles collide with one another, but otherwise they do not interact much.

Adding energy in the form of heat to a substance may result in a change of state. The added energy may cause the bonds between particles to break, which allows the state to change. Adding energy in the form of heat to a chunk of glacier may cause the ice to melt into water. Removing energy in the form of heat from a substance may also result in a change of state.

Energy Transfer

Heat flows in three main ways—conduction, convection, and radiation.

Conduction is the transfer of thermal energy as heat from one substance to another through direct contact. When objects touch each other, their particles collide. It takes place any time that objects at different temperatures come into contact with each other. When particles collide, particles with higher kinetic energy transfer energy to those with lower kinetic energy. This transfer makes some particles slow down and other particles speed up until all particles have the same average kinetic energy. Thermal conduction explains how heat flows from hot soup to a spoon placed in the soup.

A second way thermal energy is transferred is **convection**, which is the transfer of thermal energy by the movement of a liquid or a gas. In most substances as temperature increases, the density of the liquid or gas decreases. Convection occurs when a cooler, denser mass of a gas or liquid replaces a warmer, less dense mass of a gas or liquid by pushing it upward. When you boil water in a pot, the water moves in roughly circular patterns because of convection. The water at the bottom of a pot on a stove burner gets hot because it is touching the pot. As it warms, the water becomes less dense. The warmer water rises through the denser, cooler water above it. At the surface, the warm water begins to cool and become denser. The cooler water then sinks back to the bottom. It is warmed again, and the cycle continues.

A third way thermal energy is transferred is **radiation**, which is the transfer of energy by electromagnetic waves. Some examples of these waves include visible light, microwaves, and infrared light. Like conduction and convection, radiation can transfer heat from warmer to cooler objects, for example, the heat you feel when you stand next to a campfire. Unlike conduction and convection, radiation can involve either an energy

transfer between particles of matter or an energy transfer across empty space. Heat from the sun is transferred to Earth by radiation and is the most significant source of radiation that we experience on a daily basis.

Specific Heat

If you walk across a sandy beach on a hot day, you know that the sand is much hotter than the water. That is because it takes more heat to raise the temperature of the water than it does to raise the temperature of the same amount of sand. The specific heat of a substance is the quantity of energy required to raise the temperature of a unit mass by 1°C. Specific heat is a characteristic of a particular substance, regardless of its mass. Water has a higher specific heat than sand.

Student-Response Activity

1 How are heat and thermal energy related?

_____

_____

_____

2 These two blocks are placed next to each other. Draw an arrow to show the direction in which heat will flow once the blocks are set in place if block A's temperature is 60 °C and block P's temperature is 30 °C.

3 How will the temperature of a substance change when heat is added or removed?

_____

_____

_____

4 Add labels to the diagram to indicate conduction, convection, and radiation.

5 If two objects with different temperatures come into contact with each other, what happens to their temperature?

_____

_____

Benchmark Assessment SC.7.P.11.4

Fill in the letter of the best choice.

1 Which description **best** defines heat?

Ⓐ the transformation of chemical energy into light energy

Ⓑ the total energy of the particles in a sample of matter

Ⓒ the thermal energy that flows from one object to another

Ⓓ the average kinetic energy of the particles in an object

2 You hold an ice cube in your hand. Why does the ice cube feel cold to you?

Ⓕ Heat is transferred from your hand to the ice cube.

Ⓖ Heat is transferred from the ice cube to the air.

Ⓗ Cold is transferred from your hand to the ice cube.

Ⓘ Cold is transferred from the ice cube to the air.

3 Sophia places a plate of food under a lamp to keep it warm. By which method is heat transferred to the food?

Ⓐ conduction

Ⓑ convection

Ⓒ radiation

Ⓓ transformation

4 The table lists the specific heats of several common substances.

Specific Heat of Common Substances

Substance	Specific Heat (J/kg °C)
Aluminum	897
Calcium	532
Copper	385
Limestone	909

Lucas places 20 kg samples of each substance by the same heat source. All samples are at the same initial temperature. Which substance will have the **greatest** temperature after some period of time?

Ⓕ aluminum

Ⓖ calcium

Ⓗ copper

Ⓘ limestone

5 Luciana notices that the air in her science classroom is much warmer than the air in her math classroom. Which describes how the air particles are different in her colder math classroom?

Ⓐ They move faster on average.

Ⓑ They are vibrating.

Ⓒ They have less average energy.

Ⓓ They move more freely.

SC.6.P.13.1 Investigate and describe types of forces including contact forces and forces acting at a distance, such as electrical, magnetic, and gravitational.

Forces

What Is a Force?

A **force** is a push or pull. When you throw a ball, turn a page in a book, or lift a backpack, you are exerting a force. All forces are vectors, which means they have both a magnitude and a direction. A force can cause an object to accelerate, and thereby change its speed or direction of motion. The unit that measures forces is the newton (N).

Forces can also be classified as contact forces and action-at-a-distance forces. A contact force is exerted when one object touches or bumps into another. For example, a bat hitting a ball exerts a force by touching it. Friction is also a contact force. It occurs when one object is rolling, sliding, or moving through another object or material, and it opposes the motion of the object. An action-at-a distance force acts between two objects that are not necessarily touching. Magnetic, electrical, and gravitational forces are all examples of forces that act over a distance.

Electrical Forces

Two electric charges exert forces on each other over some distance. This force is called an **electric force**. Electric charges exist in two forms—negative and positive. The direction of the electric force depends on the types of charges. Like charges repel and unlike charges attract.

Magnetic Forces

Two magnets placed near one another exert a force even with space between them. The force that acts between magnetic materials is called **magnetic force**. The direction of the force depends on the positions of the magnets. Every magnet has two poles, named north (N) and south poles (S). Like poles push apart, or repel one another. Unlike poles pull together, or attract, one another.

Gravitational Forces

Gravity is a force of attraction between two objects due to their mass. Gravity is a noncontact force that acts between two objects at any distance apart. Earth's gravity pulls everything toward Earth's center. It pulls, but it does not push, so it is called an attractive force.

The magnitude of gravitational force depends on the masses of the objects and the distance between the objects. The gravitational force increases as the masses of the objects increase. So the gravitational force between Earth and the moon is greater than the gravitational force between you and your book because Earth and the moon have much greater masses.

The gravitational force decreases with the distance between two objects. That means that the gravitational force between two objects gets weaker as the objects are separated. The force gets stronger as two objects are brought closer together.

The gravitational force pulls inward toward the center of an object. So Earth's gravitational force pulls objects toward itself. This is why objects have weight. An object's weight is a measure of the pull of gravity on it. The weight depends on the gravitational force exerted on it and the mass of an object. Mass is the amount of matter in an object. The more mass an object has, the greater its weight will be.

The strength of the gravitational force differs on other planets or moons. So the weight of an object differs on other planets as well, even though its mass stays the same. Consider Earth's moon, which has gravitational pull that is about one-sixth the strength of what it is on Earth. An astronaut would weigh less on the moon than on Earth because the moon does not pull as hard on the astronaut, but has the same mass on both the moon and on Earth.

Student-Response Activity

1 Name an example of a contact force and an action-at-a-distance force.

Contact Force	Action-at-a-Distance Force
_____	_____

2 How is an action-at-a-distance force similar to a contact force? How is it different?

_____

_____

_____

_____

3 This diagram was drawn during a study of the relationship between gravitational attraction and distance.

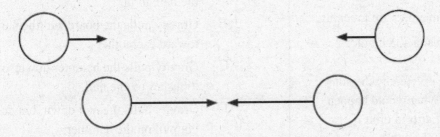

Explain what the diagram shows and what the arrows represent.

_____

_____

_____

_____

4 How can the weight of an object change if its mass remains the same? Give an example.

_____

_____

_____

_____

Benchmark Assessment SC.6.P.13.1

Fill in the letter of the best choice.

❶ Which of these forces does **not** act over a distance?

(A) electric

(B) friction

(C) gravitational

(D) magnetic

❷ Two magnets are arranged so that they pull together. Which conclusion can be reached?

(F) Two north poles are together.

(G) Two south poles are together.

(H) The poles of the magnets are touching.

(I) A north pole is near a south pole.

❸ The gravitational force exerted by the sun keeps planets in orbit. What would happen to the force that keeps Earth in orbit if Earth were farther from the sun?

(A) It would increase.

(B) It would decrease.

(C) It would disappear.

(D) It would not change.

❹ Which is a measure of force?

(F) distance

(G) mass

(H) volume

(I) weight

❺ Ignacio uses a hammer to hit a nail into a board on the floor. How does gravity make it easier to hammer the nail?

(A) Gravity pushes the board up to help the nail go in.

(B) Gravity pulls the board and the nail toward each other.

(C) Gravity pulls the hammer down so that it pushes on the nail.

(D) Gravity pulls the nail down, but does not pull on the hammer.

Name _____ Date _____

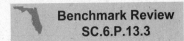

SC.6.P.13.3 Investigate and describe that an unbalanced force acting on an object changes its speed, or direction of motion, or both.

Forces and Motion

Measuring Forces

In science, a force is a push or a pull. All forces have two properties—direction and magnitude. A newton (N) is the unit used to measure the magnitude, or size, of a force. More than one force can be acting on an object at any given time. **Net force** is the combination of all of the forces acting on an object.

In diagrams, forces are often represented by arrows. The length of the arrow indicates the magnitude of the force. Consider the forces in the diagram below. The object is experiencing a force of 3 N to the left and 8 N to the right. The net force is the difference between them, 8 N – 3 N = 5 N, and it is in the direction of the greater force.

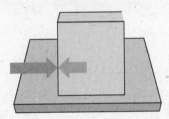

Balanced Forces

If the net force is 0 N, then the forces on an object are said to be balanced. Balanced forces will not cause a change in the motion of an object.

Individual Forces

5 N   5 N

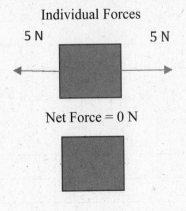

Net Force = 0 N

Many objects that have balanced forces acting on them are static, or not moving. For example, the force that you exert when you sit on a chair does not cause the chair to move. The chair does not move because the floor exerts a balancing force on the chair. An object may also be moving when balanced forces are acting on it. A car driven in a straight line at a constant speed is an example of balanced forces acting on a moving object.

Unbalanced Forces

If the net force is a nonzero value, the force is said to be unbalanced. An unbalanced force can change the velocity of an object. This change in velocity can be a change in speed, direction, or both. In other words, forces can cause acceleration.

Anytime you see a change in an object's motion, you can be sure that the change was caused by a force. Unbalanced forces can cause a static object to start moving or cause a moving object to slow down and stop moving. For example, in a soccer game, the soccer ball is already moving when one player passes it to a second player. When the ball reaches the second player, that player exerts an unbalanced force—a kick—on the ball. After the kick, the ball moves in a new direction and at a new speed.

Motion Graphs

One way to describe the motion of an object is with a distance versus time graph. The graph below represents the motion of a squirrel moving along the ground. Time, in seconds, is plotted along the horizontal axis. Distance, in meters, is plotted along the vertical axis.

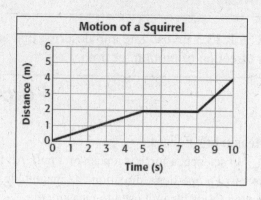
Look at the first section of the graph from 0 to 5 seconds. During this period of time, the graph shows a straight, slanted line. The line indicates that the squirrel moves at a constant speed and travels a total of 2 m. Then from 5 seconds to 8 seconds, the line is horizontal. That means that the distance stays the same at 2 m so the squirrel must have stopped moving. During the last portion of the graph, from 8 to 10 seconds, the distance is again increasing at a constant rate. The squirrel moves from 2 m to 4 m. Note that this line is steeper than the line at the beginning of the graph, which indicates that the squirrel is moving faster than it did before.

Student-Response Activity

1 A force of 6 N is exerted on an object.

Part A What could be added to this diagram so there is a net force of 10 N to the left?

_____

_____

Part B What could be added to this diagram so there is a net force of 0 N?

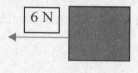

_____

_____

2 What is the net force on an object when you combine a force of 17 N north with a force of 9 N north? Be sure to include the direction of the force.

_____

_____

_____

❸ How are balanced forces different from unbalanced forces?

_____
_____
_____
_____
_____

❹ A student draws a distance verses time graph to describe the motion of a model train. What does a horizontal section of the graph indicate about the motion of the train?

_____
_____
_____
_____
_____

❺ How do you determine the net force on an object if all forces act in the same direction?

_____
_____
_____
_____
_____
_____

Benchmark Assessment SC.6.P.13.3

Fill in the letter of the best choice.

1 Maria pulls a rope to the left with a force of 12 N. Sebastian pulls on the other end of the rope to the right with a force of 7 N. Emma adds a force of 8 N, also pulling to the right. What will happen?

Ⓐ The net force will be 3 N to the right.

Ⓑ The net force will be 15 N to the left.

Ⓒ The net force will be 12 N to the right.

Ⓓ The net force will be 27 N to the left.

2 Two forces are acting on an object, but the net force on the object is 0 N. Which will cancel the two forces on the object?

Ⓕ The forces are the same size and in the same direction.

Ⓖ The forces are different sizes and in the same direction.

Ⓗ The forces are the same size and in opposite directions.

Ⓘ The forces are different sizes and in opposite directions.

3 Which causes change in speed, direction, or both?

Ⓐ balanced forces

Ⓑ unbalanced forces

Ⓒ any combination of forces

Ⓓ either balanced or unbalanced forces

4 A science class is having bug races. The graph shows the motion of a bug across the floor.

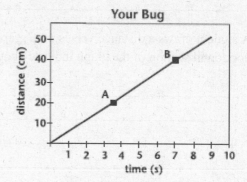

Your Bug

What happens to the bug between points A and B?

Ⓕ The bug slowed down.

Ⓖ The bug stopped moving.

Ⓗ The bug started speeding up.

Ⓘ The bug continued moving at the same speed.

5 One ball rolls along a shelf at a steady rate. A second ball rolls off the shelf and gains speed as it falls in a curved path. Which has an unbalanced force acting on it?

Ⓐ the ball that rolls along the shelf

Ⓑ the ball that falls

Ⓒ both balls

Ⓓ neither ball

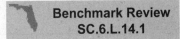
SC.6.L.14.1 Describe and identify patterns in the hierarchical organization of organisms from atoms to molecules and cells to tissues to organs to organ systems to organisms.

From Atoms to Organisms

The Smallest Units of Matter

Every object in our universe, including you, Earth, and the largest stars and galaxies, is made of the smallest of particles. The smallest unit of matter that has the properties of a substance is called an **atom**. Atoms can join together to form molecules. A **molecule** is a group of atoms held together by chemical bonds. A molecule is the smallest unit of a substance that can exist and retain all the chemical properties of the substance. Molecules form the building blocks used to produce living things. A single cell may contain millions of molecules.

The Smallest Units of Life

All living things are composed of one or more cells. A **cell** is the structural and functional unit of life. It is also the smallest unit that can carry out the activities of life. Cells have many different functions and come in many shapes and sizes. All cells are surrounded by a **cell membrane**, which is a protective layer that covers the cell's surface and acts as a barrier. It separates the cell's contents from its environment. The cell membrane also controls materials, such as water and oxygen, that move into and out of the cell. Inside the cell is a fluid and almost all of its contents, which is called the **cytoplasm**.

Cells May Work Together

In an organism made up of only one cell, different parts of the cell perform all of the functions necessary for the organism to survive. In an organism with many cells, different types of cells perform specialized functions. Organisms that are made up of many cells are called **multicellular**. Plants, animals, some protists, and many fungi are multicellular organisms.

A multicellular organism starts as a single cell. As the single cell develops into many cells, the cells become fixed into different types of cells. In a multicellular organism, such as a human, different types of cells perform different functions. These cells rely on each other and work together to do all of the activities needed for the organism to live. Such cells must be well organized in an organism. A multicellular organism can have four levels of organization: cells, tissues, organs, and organ systems.

Cells Form Tissues

A group of similar cells that perform a common function are called a **tissue**. There are four main types of tissue in the human body: muscle, epithelial, connective, and nervous. Each of these tissue types is specialized to perform certain functions. Nervous tissue functions as a messaging system within the body. Epithelial tissue is protective and forms boundaries, such as skin. Connective tissue, including bones and blood, holds parts of the body together and provides support and nourishment to organs. Muscle tissue helps produce movement.

Tissues of the same type are not necessarily identical though, and can perform different functions. For example, muscle tissue helps an organism move. Muscle tissue is also found in the heart, where it performs a very different function. The muscle tissues in your arm are both different and similar to muscle tissues in your heart.

Tissues Form Organs

One type of tissue alone cannot do all of the things that several types of tissue working together can do. A collection of tissues working together to perform a specialized function is called an **organ**. For example, your stomach is made of four types of tissue. Each tissue type can do certain things. By combining different tissues, organs can perform much more complicated tasks.

Organ Systems

You know that you need a stomach to digest food, but digestion is not a job that a stomach can do alone. Your stomach works with other organs, such as the small and large intestines, to digest your food. While individual organs can perform complicated tasks, organs working together can support even more complicated tasks that support an organism. Organs that work together to perform body functions make up an **organ system**.

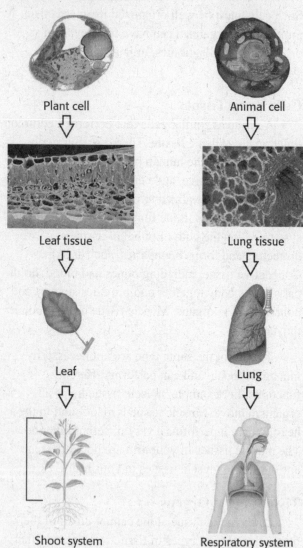

Plant cell

Animal cell

Leaf tissue

Lung tissue

Leaf

Lung

Shoot system

Respiratory system

Organisms

Organisms can be very small or very large. Regardless of size, though, every organism contains multiple parts that enable it to survive. Most of the organisms we see on a daily basis, such as trees, birds, and people, rely on multiple organ systems working together to support them. By having multiple systems each doing complicated tasks, an organism is able to act in very complicated ways. Even a simple organism, such as a blade of grass, is continuously performing complicated tasks. Feeding, for example, requires the blade of grass to use multiple organs and organ systems. A human body has an estimated 37.2 trillion cells working together! By organizing matter into ever more complex arrangements, life is able to accomplish many incredible things.

Student-Response Activity

Janet compares her school system to a living system. Use the terms in the Word Bank to fill in the first blank, and then complete the analogy by explaining which part of an organism each level within her school system is similar to for Questions 1–5.

Word Bank

cells	organ	organism	organ systems	tissue

1 Individual students are similar to _____ because _____ .

2 Classrooms are similar to _____ because _____ .

3 Each grade is similar to _____ because _____ .

4 The entire school is similar to _____ because _____ .

5 The school district is similar to _____ because _____ .

6 Look at the diagram. What level of organization is shown here? How does this level of organization relate to the cells? To organ systems?

heart

_____

_____

_____

_____

_____

_____

7 Is it possible for an organism to exist without any tissues? Explain your answer.

_____

_____

_____

Benchmark Assessment SC.6.L.14.1

Fill in the letter of the best choice.

1 You are looking through a microscope at some similar cells. Each cell has a different structure. What can you infer about these cells?

Ⓐ They have the same functions.

Ⓑ They are from different organisms.

Ⓒ They have different functions.

Ⓓ They have the same organelles.

2 Look at the diagram. What level of organization is shown in the diagram?

Ⓕ organ

Ⓖ organism

Ⓗ organ system

Ⓘ tissue

3 Which choice shows the parts of an organism arranged by size from smallest to largest?

Ⓐ atom, tissue, cell, organ

Ⓑ molecule, cell, tissue, organ

Ⓒ organ, tissue, cell, molecule

Ⓓ cell, organ, tissue, organ system

4 Some students were building a model of a digestive system. Which choice **best** describes a process they should show with their model?

Ⓕ Tissues digest food for the organ system to absorb.

Ⓖ Cells digest food, which is then absorbed by organs.

Ⓗ Organs digest food by working together as a system.

Ⓘ The organ system uses specialized cells to digest food.

5 Jenna is making a model to show how a living thing is organized. Which answer should go in section 2?

Levels of Organization of an Animal's Body

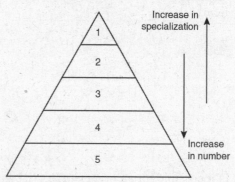

Ⓐ organs

Ⓑ organisms

Ⓒ organ systems

Ⓓ tissues

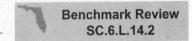
SC.6.L.14.2 Investigate and explain the components of the scientific theory of cells (cell theory): all organisms are composed of cells (single-celled or multi-cellular), all cells come from pre-existing cells, and cells are the basic unit of life.

Cell Theory

Cells

Cell theory is the scientific theory that describes how living things are made of cells. A cell is defined as the most basic structure that can carry out all of life's essential functions. These functions include taking in energy from food, eliminating waste, and reproducing to make more cells. All cells have some parts in common, including cell membranes, organelles, cytoplasm, and special molecules that carry information, called DNA.

There are two basic types of cells—cells without a nucleus and cells with a nucleus. A nucleus is the cell structure that contains a cell's genetic material. Cells without a defined nucleus are called **prokaryotic cells**. All prokaryotic organisms are single-celled organisms. Cells that have a nucleus surrounded by a membrane are called **eukaryotic cells**. Eukaryotic organisms can be single-celled or have many cells.

While all cells carry out some of the same basic functions, cells in a multicellular organism can be specialized. This means that they perform a specific task inside of an organism. These types of cells may require support by other cells in order to survive.

All Organisms Are Composed of Cells

In 1673, Anton van Leeuwenhoek, a Dutch merchant, made his own microscopes. Leeuwenhoek used one of his microscopes to look at pond scum. Leeuwenhoek saw small organisms in the water. He named these organisms *animalcules*, which means "little animals." Today, we call these single-celled organisms protists.

Leeuwenhoek also looked at animal blood. He saw differences in blood cells from different types of animals. For example, blood cells in fish, birds, and frogs are oval. Blood cells in humans and dogs are round and flat. Leeuwenhoek was also the first person to see bacteria. And he discovered that yeasts that make bread dough rise are single-celled.

Almost 200 years passed before scientists concluded that cells are present in all living things. Scientist Matthias Schleiden studied plants. In 1838, he concluded that all plant parts were made of cells. Theodor Schwann studied animals. In 1839, Schwann concluded that all animal tissues were made of cells. Soon after that, Schwann wrote the first two parts of what is now known as the **cell theory**.

- All organisms are made of one or more cells.
- The cell is the basic unit of all living things.

Later, in 1858, Rudolf Virchow, a doctor, stated that all cells could form only from other cells. Virchow then added the third part of the cell theory.

- All cells come from existing cells.

Homeostasis

We all feel more comfortable when our surroundings are ideal— not too hot, not too cold, not too wet, and not too dry. Cells are the same way. However, a cell's environment is constantly changing. **Homeostasis** is the maintenance of a constant internal state in a changing environment. In order to survive, your cells need to be able to obtain and use energy, make new cells, exchange materials, and eliminate wastes. Homeostasis ensures that cells can carry out these tasks in a changing environment.

Balance in Organisms

All cells need energy and materials in order to carry out life processes. A unicellular organism exchanges materials directly with its environment. The cell membrane and other parts of the cell regulate what materials get into and out of the cell. This is one way that unicellular organisms maintain homeostasis. Cells in multicellular organisms must work together to maintain homeostasis for the entire organism. For example, multicellular organisms have systems that transport materials to cells from other places in the organism.

The main transport system in your body is your cardiovascular system. The cardiovascular system includes the heart, blood vessels, and blood. The heart pumps blood through branched blood vessels that come close to every cell in the body. Blood carries materials to the cells and carries wastes away from the cells. Other multicellular organisms have transport systems, too. For example, many plants have two types of vascular tissues that work together as a transport system. Xylem is the tissue that transports water and minerals from the roots to the rest of the plant. Another tissue called phloem transports food made within plant cells.

Energy

Cells need energy to perform cell functions. Cells get energy by breaking down materials, such as food, in which energy is stored. Breaking down food also provides raw materials the cell needs to make other materials for cell processes.

The sun provides the energy for plants to grow and make food. Plants use sunlight to change carbon dioxide and water into sugar and oxygen. This process by which plants, algae, and some bacteria make their own food is called **photosynthesis**. Inside plant and algal cells are special organelles, called chloroplasts, where photosynthesis takes place.

All living things need food to produce energy for cell processes. The process by which cells use oxygen to produce energy from food is called **cellular respiration**. Plants, animals, and most other organisms use cellular respiration to get energy from food. Nearly all the oxygen around us is made by photosynthesis. Animals and plants use oxygen during cellular respiration to break down food. Cellular respiration also produces carbon dioxide. Plants need carbon dioxide to make sugars. So, photosynthesis and respiration are linked, each one depending on the products of the other.

Cell Division

Cells grow, divide, and die. Some cells divide more often than others. For example, cells in the skin are constantly dividing to replace those that have died or are damaged. Some cells, such as nerve cells, cannot divide to produce new cells once they are fully formed. Multicellular organisms grow by adding more cells. These new cells are made when existing cells divide.

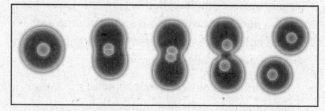

Cell division in eukaryotes is a complex process. Before a cell can divide, its DNA is copied. Then, the DNA copies are sorted into what will become two new cells. In order to divide up the DNA evenly between the new cells, the DNA needs to be packaged. The packages are called chromosomes. Equal numbers of chromosomes are separated, and the nucleus splits to form two identical nuclei. This process is called mitosis. Then, the rest of the cell divides, resulting in two identical cells. Because the two new cells have DNA identical to that found in the original cell, all the cells in an organism have the same genetic material.

Eliminating Waste

What would happen to a factory if its supply of raw materials never arrived or it could not get rid of its garbage? Like a factory, an organism must be able to obtain materials for energy, make new materials, and get rid of wastes. The exchange of materials between a cell and its environment takes place at the cell's membrane. Cell membranes are semi-permeable because they allow only certain particles to cross into or out of the cell.

The movement of particles across a cell membrane without the use of energy by the cell is called **passive transport**. For example, when a tea bag is added to a cup of water, the molecules in the tea will eventually spread throughout the water.

Cells often need to move materials across the cell membrane from areas of low concentration into areas of higher concentration. This is the opposite direction of passive transport. **Active transport** is the movement of particles against a concentration gradient and requires the cell to use energy.

Maintaining Homeostasis

As you have read, cells can obtain energy, divide, and transport materials to maintain stable internal conditions. In multicellular organisms, the cells must work together to maintain homeostasis for the entire organism. For example, when some organisms become cold, the cells respond in order to maintain a normal internal temperature. Muscle cells will contract to generate heat, a process known as shivering. Some animals adapt their behavior to control body temperature. For example, many reptiles bask in the sun or seek shade to regulate their internal temperatures. When temperatures become extremely cold, some animals hibernate. Animals such as ground squirrels are able to conserve their energy during the winter when food is scarce.

Some trees lose all their leaves around the same time each year. This is a seasonal response. Having bare branches during the winter reduces the amount of water loss. Leaves may also change color before they fall. As autumn approaches, chlorophyll, the green pigment used for photosynthesis, breaks down. As chlorophyll is lost, other yellow and orange pigments can be seen.

Student-Response Activity

1 Why do scientists consider the cell to be the basic unit of life?

_____
_____
_____
_____

2 What are the three most important functions that a cell performs?

_____
_____
_____
_____
_____

❸ Hailey makes a claim that a giant redwood tree can be grown from a single cell. Do you agree?
Explain your reasoning.

_____

_____

_____

_____

_____

❹ Describe one way that the functioning of plant cells is similar to the functioning of animal cells.

_____

_____

_____

_____

_____

❺ What does a cell have to do to maintain homeostasis?

_____

_____

_____

_____

_____

Benchmark Assessment SC.6.L.14.2

Fill in the letter of the best choice.

1 The diagram shows a plant cell and an animal cell. Which is **most likely** true about both cells?

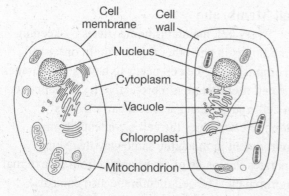

Cell membrane — Cell wall — Nucleus — Cytoplasm — Vacuole — Chloroplast — Mitochondrion

Ⓐ Both cells are single-celled organisms.

Ⓑ Both cells use the same molecules for energy.

Ⓒ Both cells have the ability to survive on their own.

Ⓓ Both cells are able to produce a complex organism.

2 Cell theory states that all living things are made out of cells. Which is **not** made of cells?

Ⓕ fingernails

Ⓖ river water

Ⓗ soil bacteria

Ⓘ tree bark

3 Suppose that a scientist discovers a new type of organism. Which can you **most likely** infer to be true?

Ⓐ The organism is either a plant or an animal.

Ⓑ The organism is made up of only one type of cell.

Ⓒ The organism has cells that are able to take in energy.

Ⓓ The organism has some cells that cannot eliminate waste.

4 Scientists observe that cells are found in every part of every organism. Which does this evidence support?

Ⓕ Cells are able to reproduce.

Ⓖ Cells are the basic unit of life.

Ⓗ Cells are able to take in energy.

Ⓘ Cells are able to get rid of waste.

5 All the cells shown are part of the same organism. Which can you infer to be true?

Ⓐ All of the cells came from the same cell.

Ⓑ All of the cells have the exact same function.

Ⓒ All of the cells have the exact same structures.

Ⓓ All of the cells are able to produce food molecules.

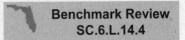

SC.6.L.14.4 Compare and contrast the structure and function of major organelles of plant and animal cells, including cell wall, cell membrane, nucleus, cytoplasm, chloroplasts, mitochondria, and vacuoles.

Structure and Function of Cells

The Cell as a Machine

Each cell requires specialized structures to perform the essential functions of life. These specialized structures, called **organelles**, are like tiny, specialized machines that help cells do certain things. Each organelle is separated from the rest of the cell by a membrane. The structure of the organelles is what allows them to do their specific jobs in the cell. Some organelles include the cell wall, cell membrane, nucleus, chloroplasts, mitochondria, and vacuoles. These organelles are found in the cytoplasm of a cell. Plant and animals cells share most of these structures.

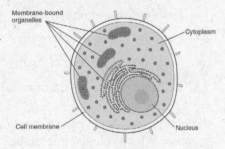

Animal Cell

Cell Wall

Plant cells have an outermost structure called a cell wall. A **cell wall** is a rigid structure that gives support to a cell. Plants and algae have cell walls made of a complex sugar called cellulose. Fungi, including yeasts and mushrooms, also have cell walls, though these cell walls are made of different materials than those of plants. Cell walls, along with vacuoles, serve to help a plant remain upright by allowing pressure to build up inside of the plant.

Cell Membrane

Every cell maintains homeostasis by keeping some things in and other things out. In order to accomplish this, the cell needs to have a membrane. The **cell membrane** is a protective layer that covers the cell's surface and acts as a barrier. This membrane separates the cell's contents from its environment in much the same way that skin separates the inside of an organism from its external environment. The cell membrane also controls materials going into and out of the cell.

Nucleus

Plant and animal cells are eukaryotic, meaning that they have a nucleus. The **nucleus** is a membrane-bound organelle, which contains the cell's DNA. Deoxyribonucleic acid, or DNA, is genetic material that provides instructions for all cell processes.

Cytoplasm

Cytoplasm is all the fluids and its contents except for the nucleus. Cytoplasm serves a similar function inside a cell to the function of blood in an organism. It carries dissolved nutrients and gasses to different parts of the cell. The cytoskeleton is a web of proteins in the cytoplasm that acts as both a muscle and a skeleton. It keeps the cell's membranes from collapsing.

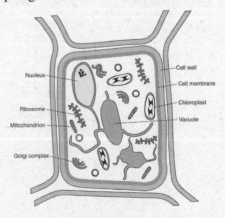

Plant Cell

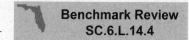
Chloroplasts

Chloroplasts are cellular organelles where photosynthesis takes place. They are found primarily in plants and bacteria. Chloroplasts are not found in animal cells. A chloroplast has two membranes. Inside of the chloroplasts, there are also smaller structures, called thylakoids. The thylakoids contain green pigment called chlorophyll. Chlorophyll appears green because it absorbs light in the red and blue regions of the sun's spectrum. The light energy absorbed by the chlorophyll can then be transferred inside of the thylakoids to molecules of carbon dioxide and water. Adding the sun's energy to these molecules allows them to form new bonds and become larger sugar molecules. These sugars are then transported to cells throughout the plant, where they are broken down again by the mitochondria.

Mitochondria

Cellular respiration takes place in an organelle called the mitochondria. Mitochondria are responsible for converting energy stored in food molecules into a form that can be used by cells. When sugar molecules pass through the cell membrane into the cell, they are sent to the mitochondria. Inside of a mitochondrion, the sugars are broken down into carbon dioxide and water. Energy is released from the bonds that had held the sugar together, and transferred to a new molecule called ATP. This process is called cellular respiration. After ATP is released from the mitochondria, it can transfer energy to different parts of the cell. Mitochondria are found in all eukaryotic cells.

Vacuoles

A vacuole is a vesicle, or a sac, that can be filled with fluid or gas. The large central vacuole in plant cells stores water and other liquids. Large central vacuoles that are full of water help support the cell. Some plants wilt when their large central vacuoles lose water. Vacuoles can also temporarily store nutrients or waste. Instead of vacuoles, animal cells have a similar structure called lysosomes. Lysosomes tend to be smaller than vacuoles in plants. They also serve different functions than plant vacuoles. Lysosomes, for example, do not support the cell's structure, but do help to break down substances inside of the cell.

Student-Response Activity

1 Plant cells contain both chloroplasts and mitochondria. Compare and contrast the functions of these organelles.

_____

_____

2 The cells of plants and animals share some—but not all—of the same organelles. What is one way that these differences in organelles explain how plants and animals are different?

_____

_____

3 Look at the diagram of a euglena cell. Early scientists were not sure how to classify this organism. What is one reason that it might be difficult to classify euglena?

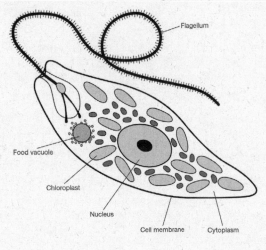

Flagellum

Food vacuole

Chloroplast

Nucleus

Cell membrane   Cytoplasm

_____

_____

_____

4 An animal ate a plant and digested sugars stored in the plant's leaves. The sugars provided energy to the animal's cells. Describe which organelles the sugar molecules must have passed through.

_____

_____

_____

Benchmark Assessment SC.6.L.14.4

Fill in the letter of the best choice.

1 Which are found in both plant and animal cells?

Ⓐ   cytoplasm and chloroplasts

Ⓑ   cell membrane and cell wall

Ⓒ   mitochondria and vacuoles

Ⓓ   large central vacuole and nucleus

2 Which choice **best** describes a plant cell?

Ⓕ   A cell that uses sugars.

Ⓖ   A cell that has a nucleus.

Ⓗ   A cell that has a cell wall.

Ⓘ   A cell that has a cell membrane.

3 What is the function of the nucleus?

Ⓐ   to hold the cell's DNA

Ⓑ   to hold the cell's organelles

Ⓒ   to hold the cell's cytoplasm

Ⓓ   to hold the cell's cell membrane

4 Which statement is true of both plant and animal cells?

Ⓕ   They do not have a rigid outermost layer.

Ⓖ   The process of obtaining energy requires sugar.

Ⓗ   Their cytoplasm contains organelles that can produce sugars.

Ⓘ   They have organelles that are each surrounded by two membranes.

5 Examine the image shown below. Which cellular organelles are **mostly** responsible for continuing this process?

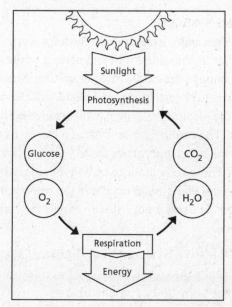

Ⓐ   the nucleus and the cell membrane

Ⓑ   the mitochondria and the chloroplasts

Ⓒ   the vacuoles and the cytoplasm

Ⓓ   the cell wall and the chloroplasts

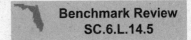

SC.6.L.14.5 Identify and investigate the general functions of the major systems of the human body (digestive, respiratory, circulatory, reproductive, excretory, immune, nervous, and musculoskeletal) and describe ways these systems interact with each other to maintain homeostasis.

Human Body Systems

Organ Systems

Your body's major organ systems work together to coordinate all the functions of the body. For example, the cardiovascular system, which includes the heart, blood, and blood vessels, works with the respiratory system, which includes the lungs. The cardiovascular system picks up oxygen from the lungs and carries the oxygen to cells in the body. These cells produce carbon dioxide, which the cardiovascular system returns to the respiratory system. The respiratory system expels the carbon dioxide.

- Digestive System: Your digestive system breaks down the food you eat into nutrients that your body can absorb.

- Respiratory System: Your lungs absorb oxygen and release carbon dioxide.

- Circulatory System: Your heart pumps blood through all of your blood vessels.

- Reproductive System: The female reproductive system produces eggs and nourishes and protects the fetus. The male reproductive system produces and delivers sperm.

- Excretory System: Your kidneys remove wastes from the blood and regulate your body's fluids.

- Immune System: The immune system returns leaked fluids to blood vessels and helps get rid of bacteria and viruses.

- Nervous System: Your brain, spinal cord, and nerves receive and send messages throughout your body.

- Musculoskeletal System: Your muscular system works with the skeletal system to help you move. Your bones provide a frame to support and protect your body parts.

Body Systems Work Together

Our body systems can do a lot, but they cannot work alone! Almost everything we need for our bodies to work properly requires many body systems to work together. For example, the nervous system may sense danger. The muscular system and skeletal system work together to help systems run away from danger.

The Nervous System

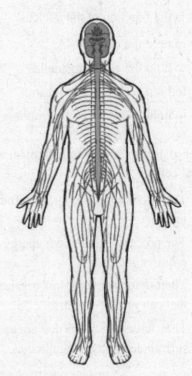

Body Systems Share Organs

Many organs are part of more than one body system. The liver works in the digestive system, but also is part of the excretory system. The heart is part of the muscular system and the cardiovascular system. Blood vessels, too, are shared. For example, blood vessels transport cells from the lymphatic and cardiovascular systems.

Body Systems Communicate

There are two basic ways cells communicate: by electrical messages and by chemical messages. Nerve cells transfer information between the body and the spinal cord and brain. Nerves pass electrical messages from one cell to the next along the line. Chemical messages are sent through the bloodstream to certain cells.

Homeostasis

Cells need certain conditions to work properly. They need food and oxygen and to have their wastes taken away. If body conditions were to change too much, cells would not be able to do their jobs. **Homeostasis** is the maintenance of a constant internal environment when outside conditions change. Responding to change allows all systems to work properly.

If one body system does not work properly, other body systems can be affected. For example, body cells that do not get enough energy or nutrients cannot work properly. A lack of food harms many systems and may cause disease or even death. The presence of toxins or pathogens also can disrupt homeostasis.

Infection

All around us, there are different microbes. Most of the time these microbes stay where they do not harm us, whether it is in our intestines or outside our bodies. Once in a while one of these infectious agents will get past our immune systems and invade our bodies. These infectious agents come in different forms, including bacteria, viruses, fungi, and parasites.

Bacteria can be found in soil, water, and even on and inside the human body. Some bacteria are necessary and helpful to humans. Other bacteria cause diseases, such as pneumonia or strep throat. Some disease-causing bacteria can directly damage cells and tissues, while others make you sick by creating toxins that harm cells. Bacterial infections can be treated with antibiotics, such as penicillin.

Viruses, which are much smaller than bacteria, cause a number of diseases, including the common cold, influenza, measles, and chicken pox. Viruses are essentially containers that hold genetic material. A virus cannot reproduce on its own so it must attach itself to a cell and insert its genetic material into the cell. Eventually, the cell will begin making more viral genetic material than its usual product. Antibiotics, which are designed to kill bacteria, have no effect on viruses. Vaccines have been developed for some viral diseases, such as the flu, measles, and chicken pox. Receiving these vaccines gives your immune system the ability to fight the viral infections on its own.

Fungi come in many forms and are usually harmless to humans. Some types of fungi can infect the human body when our immunity is low or we are on antibiotics. A yeast infection present in the mouth is caused by Candida, and it is sometimes called thrush. Other types of fungi cause skin infections such as athlete's foot. An antifungal medicine is used to treat fungal infections.

Parasitic infections are caused by a variety of different organisms. These organisms live on and receive food from the host. Human parasites can be protozoa, helminths, or ectoparasites. Protozoa are single celled and can multiply in humans. They can be transmitted orally or through getting bitten by an infected insect. Malaria is a disease caused by a protozoan which affects hundreds of millions of people. Helminths are usually large enough to be viewed without the help of a microscope and include flat worms and roundworms. Ectoparasites attach or burrow into skin and include ticks, fleas, and lice.

Name ______________________ Date ____________

Benchmark Review
SC.6.L.14.5

Student-Response Activity

Describe the general functions of these body systems in Questions 1–5:

1. Respiratory system:

2. Circulatory system:

3. Immune system:

4. Excretory system:

5. Digestive system:

6. **What is the relationship between the respiratory system and the circulatory system?**

7. **What is the reason that an antibiotic will not work on a viral infection?**

Benchmark Assessment SC.6.L.14.5

Fill in the letter of the best choice.

❶ Which **best** describes the function of the circulatory system?

(A) It is responsible for the digestion of food.

(B) It takes in oxygen and eliminates carbon dioxide.

(C) It moves oxygen and nutrients throughout the body.

(D) It transports electrical signals to different body parts.

❷ Which two systems work together to deliver nutrients to every cell of the body?

(F) digestive and excretory systems

(G) circulatory and digestive systems

(H) respiratory and nervous systems

(I) musculoskeletal and integumentary systems

❸ Groups of organs in the body work together as organ systems. Each organ system has a special role in the body. Organ systems include the nervous system, immune system, and excretory system. What is the role of the immune system in the body?

(A) It gets rid of wastes that the body produces.

(B) It uses electrical signals to control body functions.

(C) It uses chemical messages to control body functions.

(D) It gets rid of pathogens that invade the body.

❹ Which systems work together to regulate blood pressure?

(F) nervous and circulatory systems

(G) respiratory and excretory systems

(H) circular and digestive systems

(I) digestive and nervous systems

❺ Waste is removed from the blood in the kidneys. Which body system includes the kidneys?

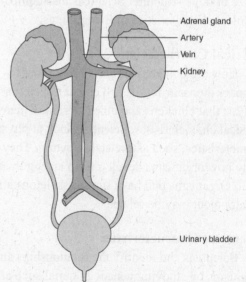

- Adrenal gland
- Artery
- Vein
- Kidney
- Urinary bladder

(A) reproductive system

(B) respiratory system

(C) immune system

(D) excretory system

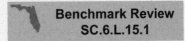

SC.6.L.15.1 Analyze and describe how and why organisms are classified according to shared characteristics with emphasis on the Linnaean system combined with the concept of Domains.

Classification of Living Things

Why We Classify

There are millions of living things on Earth. How do scientists keep all of these living things organized? Scientists classify living things based on the characteristics that living things share.

To classify organisms, scientists compare physical characteristics. For example, they may look at size or bone structure. Scientists also compare the chemical characteristics of living things.

Physical Characteristics

How are chickens similar to dinosaurs? If you compare dinosaur fossils and chicken skeletons, you will see that chickens and dinosaurs share many physical characteristics. Scientists look at physical characteristics, such as skeletal structure. They also study how organisms develop from an egg to an adult. Organisms that have similar skeletons and development may be related.

Chemical Characteristics

Scientists can identify the relationships among organisms by studying genetic material such as DNA and RNA. They use mutations and genetic similarities to find relationships among organisms. Organisms that have very similar gene sequences or have the same mutations are likely related. Other chemicals, such as proteins and hormones, can also be studied to find out how organisms are related.

The Linnaean System

The first scientist to systematically organize organisms by traits was a Swedish botanist named Carl Linnaeus. The Linnaean system of classification is still used today with some modifications. Linnaeus grouped all organisms into one of two kingdoms: Plantae and Animalia, or plants and animals. This was his highest level of organization. Below the level of kingdom, he grouped each organism into a phylum, class, order, family, genus, and species. Linnaeus was also the person who devised the system of naming organisms using *binomial nomenclature*, or by using two names as a scientific name. An organism's scientific name is made from its genus and species.

Linnaeus lived and worked in the 1700's. Since then, about 2 million new species have been described, and our understanding of the history of life has expanded greatly. As a result, the Linnaean system has necessarily had to expand as well. For Linnaeus, the kingdom was the highest level of organization. Today, scientists classify all organisms into one of three domains. Both of the kingdoms Linnaeus described, as well as two more, are contained in just one of those domains. A **domain** represents the largest differences among organisms.

Domains and Kingdoms

The three domains in the modern classification system are Archaea, Bacteria, and Eukarya. The domain **Bacteria** is made up of prokaryotes that usually have a cell wall and reproduce by cell division. Prokaryotes are single-celled organisms that lack a nucleus in their cells. Bacteria live in any environment—soil, water, and even inside the human body. Some bacteria cause diseases, such as pneumonia. Other bacteria make chemicals that help humans fight disease-causing bacteria.

The domain **Archaea** is also made up of prokaryotes. They differ from bacteria in their genetics and in the makeup of their cell walls. Archaea were first discovered living in extreme environments, such as hot springs and thermal vents, where other organisms could not survive. Some archaea can also be found in moderate environments, such as the open ocean.

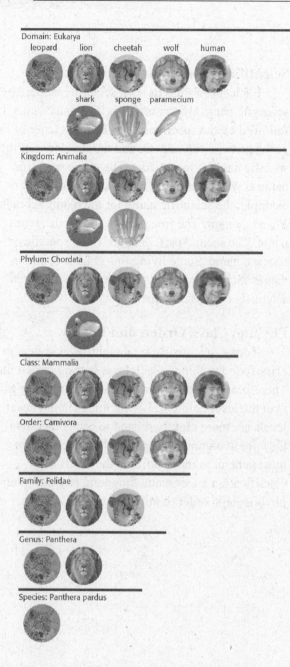

Domain: Eukarya
leopard   lion   cheetah   wolf   human
shark   sponge   paramecium

Kingdom: Animalia

Phylum: Chordata

Class: Mammalia

Order: Carnivora

Family: Felidae

Genus: Panthera

Species: Panthera pardus

All organisms that are not either bacteria or archaea are classified in the domain Eukarya. This domain is made up of all eukaryotes, or organisms made up of cells that have a nucleus and membrane-bound organelles. Four kingdoms currently make up the domain Eukarya: Protista, Fungi, Plantae, and Animalia.

• Unlike plants, fungi do not perform photosynthesis. Unlike animals, fungi do not eat food. Instead, fungi absorb nutrients from substances in their surroundings. Molds and mushrooms are examples of the complex, multicellular members of the kingdom Fungi.

• Kingdom Plantae includes organisms that are eukaryotic, have cell walls, cannot move around, and make food through photosynthesis. For photosynthesis to occur, plants must be exposed to sunlight.

• The kingdom Animalia contains complex, multicellular organisms that lack cell walls, are usually able to move around, and have specialized sense organs. They eat other organisms for food. Birds, fish, reptiles, insects, and mammals are just a few examples of animals.

• Members of the kingdom Protista, commonly called protists, are single-celled or simple multicellular organisms. Protists may have features that resemble plants, animals, fungi, or a combination of them. Algae and slime molds are both protists.

Genus and Species

Any organism that you can think of is a particular species. A **species** is a group of organisms that are very closely related and is the basic unit of classification. There are more species than there are any other levels of classification. Members of a species share all of the same characteristics, though there can be variation in those characteristics. Horses, for example, may look very different from each other, but they all share certain traits that make them different from any other organism.

Horses also share many traits with zebras. They also have many differences. Horses and zebras are members of different species, which are closely related. This makes them members of a common **genus**, or group of similar species, *Equus*.

Scientific Names

Each species has its own scientific name. The scientific name always includes the genus name followed by the specific name. The first letter of the genus name is capitalized, and the first letter of the specific name is lower case. The entire scientific name is written either in italics or underlined. For example, the scientific name for the plains zebra is *Equus quagga*. The first part, *Equus*, is the genus name. The second part, *quagga,* is the specific or species, name. Some living things have common names. Scientific names prevent confusion when scientists discuss organisms.

Phylum, Class, Order, and Family

Today, scientists use an eight-level system to classify living things. Each level gets more definite. Therefore, it contains fewer kinds of living things than the level before it. Living things in the lower levels are more closely related to each other than they are to organisms in the higher levels. From most general to most definite, the levels of classification are domain, kingdom, phylum (plural, phyla), class, order, family, genus, and species.

Student-Response Activity

1 How does the shape of a pyramid relate to the number of groups in each level of the Linnaean classification system?

_____

_____

_____

2 For which kingdom in the domain Eukarya would you most likely need a magnifying lens or microscope to study the organisms? Explain why.

_____

_____

3 What are two types of evidence used to classify organisms?

_____

_____

4 A scientist finds an organism that cannot move. It has many cells, produces spores, and gets food from its environment. In which kingdom does it belong? Explain your answer.

_____

_____

_____

5 Complete the cause-and-effect graphic organizer. Why do scientists use shared traits to make groups of related animals?

Cause:_____

_____

_____

_____

Effect: Groups of related organisms share traits.

Benchmark Assessment SC.6.L.15.1

Fill in the letter of the best choice.

1 Mike is trying to explain scientific names to a classmate. What are the two parts of a scientific name?

(A) domain and genus

(B) domain and kingdom

(C) genus and species

(D) phylum and class

2 Jelal subscribes to a nature magazine. An article about the classification of mammals included the following table.

Mammal	1	2	3
Height at shoulder	42 cm	62 cm	77 cm
Length without tail	68 cm	81 cm	110 cm
Weight	22 lb	30 lb	80 lb
Scientific name	*Canis mesomelas*	*Canis latrans*	*Canis lupus*

Based on the information in the table, which is **most likely** true?

(F) The organisms belong in the same genus.

(G) The organisms do not have a common ancestor.

(H) The organisms are members of the domain Archaea.

(I) The organisms lack common chemical characteristics.

3 Catherine knows that two different organisms are members of the same order. Which can she also infer is **true**?

(A) The organisms are members of the same species.

(B) The organisms are members of the same family.

(C) The organisms are members of the same genus.

(D) The organisms are members of the same class.

4 Victoria discovers a new organism in a pool of very hot, salty water. The cells of this organism have no nucleus. Which is **most likely** true?

(F) It is a member of the domain Bacteria.

(G) It is a member of the domain Archaea.

(H) It is a member of the kingdom Protista.

(I) It is a member of the kingdom Animalia.

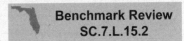
SC.7.L.15.2 Explore the scientific theory of evolution by recognizing and explaining ways in which genetic variation and environmental factors contribute to evolution by natural selection and diversity of organisms.

The Scientific Theory of Evolution

Life on Earth Changes

Life first appeared on Earth nearly 4 billion years ago. Since then, many species—such as dinosaurs—appeared, survived for a time, and then died. An incredible diversity of life exists because species have changed over time, or evolved. In biology, **evolution** refers to the process in which populations gradually change over time. If a species cannot adapt to its changing environment, the species will become extinct. **Extinction** is when all the members of a species have died. For example, changing climate conditions at the end of the Ice Age was one contributing factor to the extinction of the wooly mammoth.

Scientists observe that species have changed over time. They also observe that the inherited characteristics in populations change over time. Sometimes a population changes so much that it can no longer reproduce with the rest of the species. That population becomes a new species. An early form of a species, called an *ancestor*, may give rise to many new *descendent* species over time. As populations change over time, new species form. Thus, newer species descend from older species.

Natural Selection

In 1859, Charles Darwin proposed the theory that evolution happens through natural selection. **Natural selection** is the process by which organisms that inherit advantageous traits tend to reproduce more successfully than the other organisms do. There are four main parts of the natural selection process—overproduction, genetic variation, selection, and adaptation.

Overproduction is a way of saying that not all organisms will survive. When a plant or animal reproduces, it usually makes more offspring than the environment can support. For example, a female jaguar may have up to four pups. Only some of them will survive to adulthood, and a smaller number of them will successfully reproduce.

Genetic variation means that not all organisms will be exactly the same. Within a species there are natural differences, or **variations**, in traits. Genetic variations can be passed on from parent to offspring. Sometimes a mutation occurs that changes genetic material. As each new generation is produced, new genetic differences may be introduced into a population. In this way, genetic variations can add up in a population. The more genetic variation a population has, the more likely it is that some individuals might have traits that will be advantageous if the environment changes.

Selection occurs when certain traits help some animals survive better than other animals. Individuals try to get the resources they need to survive. These resources include food, water, space and, in most cases, mates for reproduction. About 11,000 years ago jaguars faced a shortage of food because the climate changed and many species died. A genetic variation in jaw size became important for survival. Jaguars with larger jaws could eat hard-shelled reptiles when other prey was hard to find.

Darwin reasoned that individuals with a particular trait, like a large jaw, are more likely to survive long enough to reproduce. As a result, the trait is "selected," or becomes more common in the next generation of offspring.

An adaptation is an inherited trait that helps an organism survive and reproduce in its environment. A larger jaw helped jaguars survive when food was hard to find. As natural selection repeats from generation to generation, these adaptations become more common in the population, and new adaptations may arise. Over time, the population becomes better adapted to the environment.

Extinction

What happens when the environment that a species has adapted to changes? The environmental change could be gradual, or it could happen suddenly. Changes in environmental conditions can affect the survival of individuals with a particular trait. The species may be able to survive at first. But, if no individuals were born with traits that help them to survive and reproduce in the changed environment, the species will become extinct.

Extinction is when all of the members of a species have died. Competition, new predators, and the loss of habitat are environmental pressures that can limit the growth of populations and could lead to extinction.

Fossil Evidence

Scientists observe that all living organisms have characteristics in common, and inherit characteristics in similar ways. Evidence of common ancestry can be found in fossils and in living organisms.

All of the fossils that have been discovered make up the **fossil record**. The fossil record provides evidence about the order in which species have existed through time, and how they have changed over time. By examining the fossil record, scientists can learn about the history of life on Earth.

Fossils found in newer layers of Earth's crust tend to have physical or molecular similarities to present-day organisms. These similarities indicate that the fossilized organisms were close relatives of the present-day organisms. Fossils from older layers are less similar to present-day organisms than fossils from newer layers are. Most older fossils are of earlier life-forms such as dinosaurs, which do not exist anymore.

Scientists examine the fossil record to figure out the relationship between extinct and living organisms. They have named and described millions of living and ancient species. Scientists use information about these species to sketch out a diverse "tree of life" that includes all known organisms.

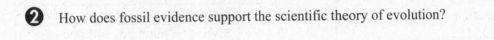
Student-Response Activity

❶ How can an adaptation help an organism produce more offspring?

_____

_____

_____

❷ How does fossil evidence support the scientific theory of evolution?

_____

_____

_____

❸ How can natural selection account for the long necks of giraffes?

_____

_____

_____

❹ Why might a species go extinct?

_____

_____

_____

❺ Suppose the climate in a specific location becomes warmer. What are two things that might happen to a mammal species with a thick fur coat that lives in this location?

_____

_____

_____

Benchmark Assessment SC.7.L.15.2

Fill in the letter of the best choice.

1 Which is **least likely** to cause a species to become extinct due to environmental changes?

(A) less genetic variation

(B) more genetic variation

(C) specific food preferences

(D) more competition for food

2 When do genetic changes occur in a population of organisms?

(F) when the organisms become extinct

(G) when the organisms produce offspring

(H) when the organisms find a new food source

(I) when the organisms interact with another species

3 Which will **most likely** happen to a species that cannot adapt to a changing environment?

(A) The species will reproduce.

(B) The species will become extinct.

(C) The species will learn a new behavior.

(D) The species will continue to live in the same location.

4 Ronald observes a sparrow's nest in a shrub outside his home. The table below describes his findings.

Week	Observations
1	Six eggs were laid in the nest.
3	Five eggs hatched, and one egg did not hatch.
4	One of the chicks disappeared.
7	Three of the chicks learned to fly, and another one disappeared.

What part of natural selection did Ronald observe?

(F) adaptation

(G) overproduction

(H) selection

(I) variation

5 Environmental changes may lead to the evolution of a species. Polar bears live in the Arctic. Ice in the Arctic is melting fast, reducing the range where the polar bear can live. If the population of polar bears does not have adaptations that allow them to survive these changes, what may happen to them?

(A) They may become extinct.

(B) They may overpopulate.

(C) They may change the environment.

(D) They may become another species.

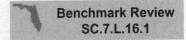
SC.7.L.16.1 Understand and explain that every organism requires a set of instructions that specifies its traits, that this hereditary information (DNA) contains genes located in the chromosomes of each cell, and that heredity is the passage of these instructions from one generation to another.

Heredity

Genotypes and Phenotypes

About 150 years ago, Gregor Mendel discovered the principles of heredity while studying pea plants. **Heredity** is the passing of information and traits from parents to offspring. Mendel knew from his experiments with plants that there must be two sets of instructions for each trait an organism inherits. The first-generation plants carried the instructions for the next generation's traits. Scientists now call these instructions for inherited traits genes. Each parent gives one set of genes to the offspring. The offspring then has two forms of the same gene for every characteristic, or feature, one from each parent. The different forms (often dominant and recessive) of a gene are called **alleles**. The information carried by genes is encoded by a special molecule called **DNA**.

DNA

The cells of all living things contain the molecule deoxyribonucleic acid, or DNA. DNA is the genetic material of living things, and carries instructions for the organism's traits. When organisms reproduce, they pass copies of their DNA to their offspring. Passing DNA ensures that the traits of parents are passed to the offspring. This passing of traits is heredity. **Genes** are segments of DNA found in chromosomes that give instructions for producing a certain characteristic. Humans, similar to other organisms, inherit their genes from their parents.

Scientists recognize that the material that makes up genes must be able to do two things. First, it must be able to give instructions for building and maintaining cells. Second, it must be able to be copied each time a cell divides so that each cell contains identical genes. The structure of DNA allows for these two functions to occur.

Because cells have two copies of each chromosome, they also have two copies of each gene. These copies may be the same allele or different alleles. If a cell has two different alleles, what trait will the cell have? It depends on whether the alleles are dominant or recessive. If a cell has a dominant allele and a recessive allele, the cell will have the trait specified by the dominant allele.

For example, consider the gene responsible for producing dimples, or creases in the cheeks. This gene comes in two alleles: one for dimples and one for no dimples. If you have even one copy of the allele for dimples, you will have dimples. This happens because the allele for producing dimples is dominant. The dominant allele contributes to the phenotype if one or two copies are present in the genotype. The no-dimples allele is recessive. The recessive allele contributes to the phenotype only when two copies of it are present.

Punnett Squares and Pedigrees

A **Punnett square** is a graphic used to predict the possible genotypes of offspring in a given cross. A Punnett square models how dominant and recessive traits may be passed from parents to offspring. Scientists can use Punnett squares to predict the probability of how often certain traits will appear in the offspring. In a Punnett square, dominant alleles are often shown with a capital letter, while recessive alleles are shown with a lowercase letter.

	Mother	
	H	**h**
h	Hh	hh
h	Hh	hh

Father (label on left side)

A Punnett square does not tell you what the exact results of a certain cross will be. A Punnett square only helps you find the probability that a certain genotype will occur. **Probability** is the mathematical chance of a specific outcome in relation to the total number of possible outcomes. Probability can be expressed in the form of a **ratio**, which is an expression that compares two quantities. A ratio written as 1:4 is read as "one to four." The ratios obtained from a Punnett square tell you the probability that any one offspring will get certain alleles. Another way of expressing probability is as a percentage. A percentage is like a ratio that compares a number to 100. A percentage states the number of times a certain outcome might happen out of a hundred chances.

A pedigree is another tool used to study patterns of inheritance. A **pedigree** traces the occurrence of a trait through generations of a family. Pedigrees can trace any inherited trait—such as hair color. Squares in a pedigree represent males, and circles represent females. A horizontal line between a square and a circle represents a pair of parents. Vertical lines down connect parents to offspring.

A pedigree can trace diseases, such as sickle cell anemia. Sickle cell anemia is caused by red blood cells that have a curved sickle shape instead of a round one. Carriers of the disease have one recessive allele. They will produce both sickle-shaped and round red blood cells. Because they have some unaffected blood cells, they will not develop the disease. They are, however, able to pass the recessive allele on to their children.

Individuals with two different alleles of a gene are **heterozygous** for that gene. Carriers are shown in the pedigree by a square or circle that is half shaded. If a child receives a recessive allele from each parent, then the child will have sickle cell anemia. Individuals with two identical copies of a single gene are **homozygous** for that gene. People with the disease are shown by a fully shaded square or circle. Other genetic conditions follow a similar pattern.

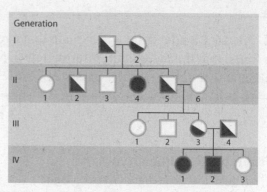

Generation

Sexual and Asexual Reproduction

There are two kinds of reproduction: asexual and sexual. Asexual reproduction results in offspring with genotypes that are exact copies of their parent's genotype. Sexual reproduction produces offspring that share traits with their parents, but are not exactly like either parent.

In sexual reproduction, two parent cells join together to form offspring that are different from both parents. The parent cells are called sex cells. Sex cells are different from ordinary body cells. Sex cells are produced by a process called meiosis. **Meiosis** is a copying process that produces cells with half the usual number of chromosomes. Human body cells, for example, have 23 pairs of chromosomes, for a total of 46. But human sex cells only have 23 chromosomes—half the usual number. Sexual reproduction occurs when sex cells from the two parents join together. The new cell that forms when an egg cell and a sperm cell join has 46 chromosomes.

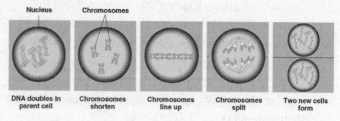

Nucleus	Chromosomes			
DNA doubles in parent cell	Chromosomes shorten	Chromosomes line up	Chromosomes split	Two new cells form

In asexual reproduction, only one parent cell is needed. The structures inside the cell are copied, and then the parent cell divides, making two exact copies. This type of cell reproduction is known as **mitosis**. Most of the cells in your body and most single-celled organisms reproduce in this way.

Name _____ Date _____

Student-Response Activity

The pedigree shows the pattern of inheritance for a disease in a family. Use it to answer Questions 1-2.

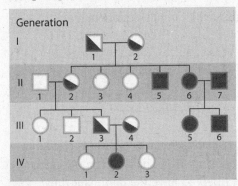

1 How many people in each of the generations have the disease?

Generation I _____   Generation III _____

Generation II _____   Generation IV _____

2 Of the total alleles in this family, how many are the diseased allele? Explain your reasoning.

_____

_____

_____

_____

3 Fill in the genotypes in the Punnett square below.

	T	t
T		
t		

4 Write the probabilities of each genotype for the Punnett square above.

TT _____   Tt _____   tt _____

5 Explain the difference between sexual reproduction and asexual reproduction.

_____

_____

_____

6 Yellow color in peas is dominant to green color. Could two yellow pea plants produce green offspring? Explain your answer.

_____

_____

_____

Benchmark Assessment SC.7.L.16.1

Fill in the letter of the best choice.

1 Noriko is studying a plant species she found in a forest. She collects leaf samples from a parent plant, and from the smaller offspring growing next to it. After running some tests, she finds that the offspring are genetically identical to the parent plant. Which is **true** about Noriko's find?

(A) The offspring were produced sexually, and two parents were required.

(B) The offspring were produced asexually; two parents were required.

(C) The offspring were produced sexually; only one parent was required.

(D) The offspring were produced asexually; only one parent was required.

2 A species of rabbit can have brown fur or white fur. One rabbit with two alleles for brown fur (*BB*) has brown fur. A second rabbit with two alleles for white fur (*bb*) has white fur. Which is **true** about the alleles *B* and *b*?

(F) They are on two different genes.

(G) They result in the same phenotype.

(H) They are two different versions of the same gene.

(I) They provide identical instructions for a characteristic.

3 Which statement **best** describes DNA?

(A) It can be found in every living cell.

(B) It can be found only in specialized cells.

(C) It can be found only in cells with a nucleus.

(D) It can be found only when cells are dividing.

4 Examine the Punnett square below.

	R	r
R	RR	Rr
r	Rr	rr

A cross between the two parents results in 50 offspring. How many of the offspring are **most likely** to have the dominant trait?

(F) 12

(G) 25

(H) 30

(I) 38

5 Which describes two things that DNA does to make life possible?

(A) It provides energy to cells and survives a cell's death.

(B) It copies itself and gives instructions for building cells.

(C) It copies itself and changes in response to the environment.

(D) It provides energy to cells and passes from parents to offspring.

6 Which trait will an organism that receives one dominant gene and one recessive gene **most likely** have?

(F) The organism will have the dominant trait.

(G) The organism will have the recessive trait.

(H) The organism will not have either trait.

(I) There is not enough information to tell what the phenotype will be.

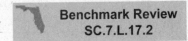
SC.7.L.17.2 Compare and contrast the relationships among organisms, such as mutualism, predation, parasitism, competition, and commensalism.

Relationships Among Organisms

All Living Things Are Connected

The web of life connects all organisms to each other and to the environment. Organisms need energy and matter for life. Interactions between organisms allow the exchange of energy and matter to occur. Ecology is the study of how organisms interact with one another and with the environment.

Predation

Every organism lives with and affects other organisms. Many organisms must feed on other organisms to get the energy and nutrients they need to survive. These feeding relationships establish structure within a community.

Many interactions between species consist of one organism eating another. An animal that is eaten is called the **prey**. The organism that eats the prey is called the **predator**. When a bird eats a worm, the worm is prey, and the bird is the predator.

Symbiosis

Many organisms in nature form associations with each other. Such a relationship is called **symbiosis**. Symbiotic relationships are always beneficial to at least one organism, but may not be for the other. Often, one organism lives in or on the other organism. Symbolic relationships are classified as mutualism, commensalism, and parasitism.

A symbolic relationship in which both organisms benefit is called **mutualism**. An example of this is the relationship between bees and flowers. The bees gather nectar from the flower and while doing so, pollen attaches to their bodies. They transport this pollen to other flowers, which pollinates them. Without bees some types of plants would not get pollinated. Neither organism is harmed in this relationship.

A relationship between two organisms in which one benefits and the other is uneffected is called **commensalism**. An example of this is barnacles that attach to scallop shells. The barnacles gain a place to live while not harming or helping the scallop. Some examples of commensalism involve protection. For example, certain shrimp live among the spines of the fire urchin. The fire urchin's spines are poisonous, but not to the shrimp. By living among the urchin's spines, the shrimp are protected from predators. In this relationship, the shrimp benefits and the fire urchin is unaffected.

A symbiotic association in which one organism benefits while the other is harmed is called **parasitism.** The organism that benefits is called the parasite. The organism that is harmed is called the host. The parasite gets nourishment from its host while the host is weakened. Sometimes, a host dies. Parasites, such as ticks, live outside the host's body. Other parasites, such as tapeworms, live inside the host's body.

Competition

In a biological community, organisms compete for resources. **Competition** occurs when organisms fight for the same limited resource. Organisms compete for resources such as food, water, sunlight, shelter, and mates. If an organism does not get all the resources it needs, it could die. Sometimes competition happens among individuals of the same species. For example, different groups of lions compete with each other for living space. Males within these groups also compete with each other for mates. Competition can also happen among individuals of different species. Lions mainly eat large animals, such as zebras. They compete for zebras with leopards and cheetahs. When zebras are scarce, competition increases among animals that eat zebras. As a result, lions may steal food or compete with other predators for smaller animals.

Food Webs

Energy is all around us. The energy from food is chemical in the bonds of food molecules. All living things need a source of chemical energy to survive. A **producer** uses energy to make food.

Most producers use sunlight to make food in a process called photosynthesis. Most producers are plants, but algae and some bacteria are also producers. Algae are the main producers in the ocean. The food that producers make supplies the energy for other living things.

Organisms that eat other organisms are called **consumers**. Consumers eat producers or other animals to obtain energy because they cannot make their own food. A consumer that eats only plants is called an **herbivore**. A **carnivore** is a consumer that eats animals. An **omnivore** eats both plants and animals. Scavengers are omnivores that eat dead plants and animals.

Organisms that get energy by breaking down dead organisms are called **decomposers**. Bacteria and fungi are decomposers. These organisms remove stored energy from dead organisms. They produce simple materials, such as water and carbon dioxide, which can be used by other living things. Decomposers are nature's recyclers.

Organisms change energy from the environment or from their food into other types of energy. Some of this energy is used for the organism's activities, such as breathing or moving. Some of the energy is saved within the organism to use later. If an organism is eaten or decomposes, the consumer or decomposer takes in the energy stored in the original organism. Only chemical energy that an organism has stored in its tissues is available to consumers. In this way, energy is transferred from organism to organism.

A **food chain** is the path of energy transfer from producers to consumers. Energy moves from one organism to the next in one direction. The arrows in a food chain represent the transfer of energy, as one organism is eaten by another. Arrows represent the flow of energy from the body of the

consumed organism to the body of the consumer of that organism. Producers form the base of food chains. Producers transfer energy to the first, or primary, consumer in the food chain. The next, or secondary, consumer in the food chain consumes the primary consumer. A tertiary consumer eats the secondary consumer. Finally, decomposers recycle matter back to the soil.

Few organisms eat just one kind of food. So, the energy and nutrient connections in nature are more complicated than a simple food chain. A **food web** is the feeding relationships among organisms in an ecosystem. Food webs are made up of many food chains.

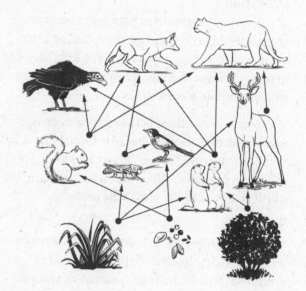

Limiting Factors

Populations cannot grow without stopping, because the environment contains a limited amount of food, water, living space, and other resources. Because there is a limited amount of resources in any ecosystem, communities of organisms are in competition with each other. Plants, for example, have to compete for space and access to sunlight. Animals that eat the same foods compete for food resources. Animals may also compete for territory or access to mates. Having enough space to spread out also helps prevent the spread of disease and parasites in a community. Disease and parasites can also act as limiting factors by reducing survival rates in a community.

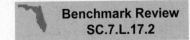
A **limiting factor** is an environmental factor that keeps a population from reaching its full potential size. For example, food becomes a limiting factor when a population becomes too large for the amount of food available. Any single resource can be a limiting factor to a population's size. The largest population that an environment can support is known as the carrying capacity. When a population grows larger than its carrying capacity, limiting factors in the environment cause individuals to die off or leave. As individuals die or leave, the population decreases.

One factor limits a population at a time. Suppose the area that had only enough food for 500 armadillos suddenly had enough food for 2,000 armadillos, but only enough water for 1,000 armadillos. The population still couldn't grow to 2,000 armadillos. Water would keep the population at 1,000 armadillos. In this case, water is the limiting factor.

Student-Response Activity

Identify each relationship as mutualism, predation, parasitism, competition, or commensalism for Questions 1–5.

❶ _____ Fleas are living on a dog and feeding of the dog's blood.

❷ _____ Pseudoscorpions hide under the wings of large beetles. The pseudoscorpions are transported to far areas while not harming the beetles.

❸ _____ Bacteria in an animal's intestines help the animal digest food while getting food at the same time.

❹ _____ A lion eats a zebra.

❺ _____ Plants need nitrogen from the soil. One plant has faster growing roots and is able to absorb nitrogen faster than its slow growing neighbors, causing the other plants to die.

Use the food web diagram to answer Questions 6–8.

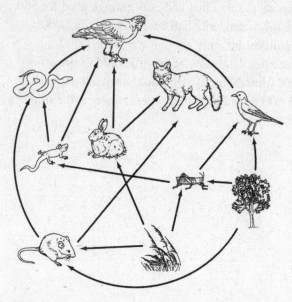

6 Which organisms are producers in this food web?

_____

_____

_____

7 What might happen to the rabbit population if the hawk population declined?

_____

_____

_____

_____

8 Which organism in the food web do you think would have the biggest impact if it were removed from the ecosystem? Explain your answer.

_____

_____

_____

_____

_____

_____

Benchmark Assessment SC.7.L.17.2

Fill in the letter of the best choice.

❶ Under what conditions are resources such as water, food, or sunlight likely to be limiting factors?

(A) when population size is decreasing

(B) when predators eat their prey

(C) when the population is small

(D) when a population is approaching the carrying capacity

❷ Suppose that humans introduce rabbits into an area where rabbits have no natural predators. Which **best** predicts what would happen?

(F) The rabbits would be killed by a new predator.

(G) The rabbits would die off because they have no food.

(H) The rabbits would fit into the ecosystem without disturbing it.

(I) The rabbits would thrive and decrease the producer population.

❸ Which **best** describes a food web?

(A) Many individual organisms of the same species live in the same space and share resources.

(B) A black bear eats fruit and then spreads the fruit's seeds through its excretions.

(C) All life is connected by the transfer of energy and nutrients among organisms and their environment.

(D) An ecosystem is made up of a community of organisms and their environment.

❹ Look at the diagram of the Arctic food web. Which describes competition shown in the food web?

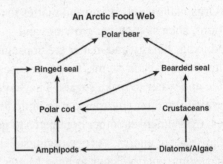

An Arctic Food Web

(F) The bearded seal and the ringed seal compete over polar bears.

(G) The polar cod and the bearded seal compete for the crustaceans.

(H) The polar cod and the crustaceans compete for the diatoms/algae.

(I) The bearded seal and the crustaceans compete for the diatoms/algae.

❺ Which best describes the flow of energy in the arctic food web?

(A) amphipods to diatoms to polar cod to polar bear

(B) diatoms to crustaceans to bearded seal to polar bear

(C) polar bear to bearded seal to crustaceans to diatoms

(D) polar cod to crustaceans to bearded seal to polar bear

SC.8.L.18.4 Cite evidence that living systems follow the Laws of Conservation of Mass and Energy.

Matter and Energy Transfer

Laws of Conservation of Mass and Energy

Organisms need energy and matter for many functions, such as moving, growing, and reproducing. Energy and matter are constantly moving through ecosystems. Producers use carbon dioxide and water to make sugars. They collect materials from their environment to build their bodies. Consumers eat other organisms to get food that they use for energy. As one organism eats another, some energy is lost as heat. Matter is returned to the physical environment as wastes or when organisms die.

The law of conservation of energy states that energy cannot be created or destroyed. Energy changes forms. Producers change light energy from the sun to chemical energy in sugars. When sugars are used, some energy is given off as heat. Much of the energy in sugars is changed to another form of chemical energy that cells can use for life functions. The **law of conservation of mass** states that mass cannot be created or destroyed. Instead, matter moves through the environment in different forms.

Ecosystems do not have clear boundaries, so energy and matter can leave them. Matter and energy can leave an ecosystem when organisms move. For example, some birds feed on fish in the ocean. When birds fly back to land, they take the matter and energy from the fish out of the ocean. Matter and energy can leave ecosystems by drifting down rivers or by being blown by the wind. Even though the matter and energy leave an ecosystem, they are never destroyed.

Photosynthesis

Nearly all life on Earth gets energy from the sun. Plants make food with the energy from the sun. So, they use this energy directly. In a process called **photosynthesis**, plants use energy from sunlight, carbon dioxide and water to make sugar. Plants capture light energy from the sun and change it to chemical energy in sugars. In addition to sugars, photosynthesis also produces oxygen gas.

Photosynthesis takes place in a plant cell's chloroplasts, such as the one shown below. Chloroplasts have two membranes and their own DNA. Chloroplasts are green because they contain chlorophyll, a green pigment. Chlorophyll is found in an internal membrane system within a chloroplast. Chlorophyll traps the energy of sunlight. This energy is used to make sugar. The chemical reaction for photosynthesis is:

$$6CO_2 + 6H_2O + energy \rightarrow C_6H_{12}O_6 + 6O$$

Chloroplast

Cellular Respiration

What do organisms do with the sugars produced through photosynthesis? They need to break the sugars down so their bodies are able to use them. The process of breaking down sugars, such as glucose, into carbon dioxide and water is called **cellular respiration**. Through cellular respiration, the energy stored in the bonds between the atoms in a sugar molecule is transferred to a new molecule called adenosine triphosphate (ATP). ATP powers many of the chemical reactions that enable cells to survive. When the bonds of ATP break, energy is released.

All cellular processes require ATP. Most of cellular respiration occurs in the mitochondria of cells. All living organisms can use cellular respiration. The chemical reaction for cellular respiration is:

$$C_6H_{12}O_6 + 6O_2 \rightarrow 6CO_2 + 6H_2O + \text{chemical energy}$$

(glucose + oxygen → carbon dioxide + water + energy)

The Carbon Cycle

Carbon is an important building block of organisms. It is found in sugars, which store the chemical energy that organisms need to live. Carbon is also found in the atmosphere (as carbon dioxide gas), in bodies of water, in rocks and soils, in organisms and in fossil fuels. Matter and energy move through organisms and between organisms and the physical environment in the **carbon cycle**.

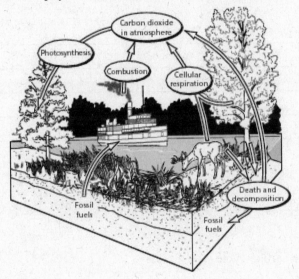

During photosynthesis, producers in the water and on land take in light energy from the sun and use carbon dioxide and water to make sugars. These sugars contain carbon and store chemical energy. Oxygen gas is also a product of photosynthesis.

Cellular respiration occurs in producers and consumers on land and in water. During respiration, sugars are broken down to release energy. The process uses oxygen gas. Carbon dioxide, water, and heat are released.

Combustion is the burning of once living materials, including wood and fossil fuels. This releases carbon dioxide, water, heat energy, and other materials into the environment. It may also produce pollution.

Decomposition is the breakdown of dead organisms and wastes. Decomposers get energy from this material by respiration. Decomposition returns carbon dioxide, water, and other nutrients to the environment.

Student-Response Activity

1 How does the carbon cycle obey the Law of Conservation of Mass?

_____

_____

2 In your own words, explain the process of photosynthesis.

_____

_____

_____

_____

_____

3 How is matter transferred in the carbon cycle?

_____

_____

_____

_____

4 Finish this equation for cellular respiration:

Glucose + Oxygen → _____ + water +
energy

5 Add the missing phrase to complete the model of the carbon cycle.

Carbon dioxide is in the atmosphere.

↓

_____

↓

Herbivores consume producers.

↓

Decomposers break down herbivores.

Benchmark Assessment SC.8.L.18.4

Fill in the letter of the best choice.

1 Why is photosynthesis important to consumers?

- (A) Consumers use oxygen and glucose produced by photosynthesis.
- (B) Consumers supply the light energy needed for photosynthesis.
- (C) Consumers supply the water needed for photosynthesis.
- (D) Consumers supply the chloroplasts to producers.

2 Where does energy first come into an ecosystem?

- (F) Producers make energy.
- (G) The sunlight provides energy to producers.
- (H) Consumers obtain energy from animals.
- (I) Scavengers obtain energy from dead plants.

3 How does carbon dioxide in the atmosphere eventually cycle through to a carnivore?

- (A) Plants use carbon dioxide in the atmosphere during photosynthesis, herbivores eat the plants, and a carnivore eats an herbivore.
- (B) Carnivores use carbon dioxide in the atmosphere during cellular respiration.
- (C) Herbivores use carbon dioxide during photosynthesis, and a carnivore eats an herbivore.
- (D) Plants use carbon dioxide in the atmosphere during photosynthesis, and a carnivore eats the plants.

4 How do plants convert glucose to energy?

- (F) through photosynthesis
- (G) when an animal consumes them
- (H) through cellular respiration
- (I) They do not convert glucose to energy.

5 Miriam is constructing a model of the carbon cycle. Which components should she include in her model?

- (A) the sun, the atmosphere, and the ocean
- (B) fossil fuels, power plants, and electricity
- (C) the atmosphere, decomposers, and the geosphere
- (D) the atmosphere, the geosphere, and the cryosphere

FSSA Practice Test–Form A

Instructions–Form A

The following pages contain a practice test. Do not look at the test until your teacher tells you to begin.

Use the answer sheet on page 178 to mark your answers.

Read each question carefully. Restate the question in your own words.

Watch for key words such as **best, not, most, least** and **except**.

A question might include one or more tables, graphs, diagrams, or pictures. Study these carefully before choosing an answer.

For questions 1–60, find the best answer. Fill in the answer bubble for that answer.

Do not make any stray marks around answer spaces.

1 In multicellular organisms, cells are arranged into groups that work together to perform a common function. What are these groups called?

   A   bones

   B   joints

   C   systems

   D   tissues

2 Plants also have organs that are made up of different tissues working together. Which is an example of a plant organ?

   F   chlorophyll

   G   leaf

   H   root system

   I   shoot system

3 Kayla summarizes cell theory to her class. She states that all organisms are made up of one or more cells. Which correctly completes her summary?

   A   All cells come from existing cells, and all cells have the same parts.

   B   All cells are the same size, and the cell is the basic unit of all organisms.

   C   The cell is the basic unit of all organisms, and all cells come from existing cells.

   D   The cell is the basic unit of all organisms, and all cells have the same parts.

4 It is important to survival that both unicellular and multicellular organisms are able to maintain homeostasis. Which is **not** an example of how organisms maintain homeostasis?

   F   Cells always stay the same.

   G   Cell division allows organisms to grow and repair damaged parts.

   H   Food is made during photosynthesis, and energy is produced from food during respiration.

   I   Materials move into and out of cells through the cell membrane.

5 Cecilia finds this cell under the microscope:

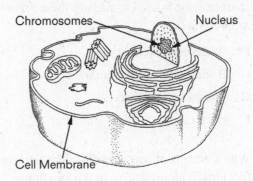

   How does she know it is an animal cell?

   A   It does not have a cell wall.

   B   It has a cell membrane.

   C   It has a nucleus.

   D   It is round.

6 Organ systems work together to meet the needs of the human body. How is the skeletal system related to the nervous system?

   F   The brain and spinal cord hold the skeleton together.

   G   The brain determines how the skeleton develops.

   H   The skeleton protects the brain and spinal cord.

   I   The skeletal system works as a part of the nervous system.

7 Some diseases cause a person's kidneys to not function properly. A dialysis machine is a device that does the work of a person's kidneys. What does a dialysis machine do?

   A   breaks down nutrients

   B   delivers oxygen to the blood

   C   filters waste from the blood

   D   regulates the digestive system

8 Bacteria belong to the domain Bacteria. Which characteristic is used to classify these organisms as Bacteria?

   F Bacteria are heterotrophs.

   G Bacteria are multicellular.

   H Bacteria are prokaryotes.

   I Bacteria cells contain a nucleus.

9 Which statement correctly describes the way that almost all organisms in the kingdoms Plantae and Animalia obtain nutrients?

   A Plants are autotrophs, and animals are heterotrophs.

   B Plants are heterotrophs, and animals are autotophs.

   C Both plants and animals are autotrophs.

   D Both plants and animals are heterotrophs.

10 Epiphytic plants, such as orchids and some ferns, grow in the canopy of trees. The epiphytic plants get the benefit of more sunlight and rain while not harming the trees. What relationship do epiphytic plants and trees have?

   F commensalism

   G mutualism

   H parasitism

   I predator-prey

11 Matter and energy can neither be created nor destroyed. What happens to energy and matter when an organism is eaten?

   A Energy and matter are moved to the ocean.

   B Energy and matter are released into the atmosphere.

   C Energy and matter are stored as fossil fuels.

   D Energy and matter move to the consumer.

12 This diagram shows the process of photosynthesis.

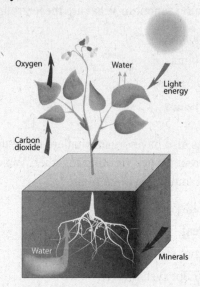

Which substance is a product of photosynthesis?

   F carbon dioxide

   G light energy

   H minerals

   I oxygen

13 In winter, flocks of birds made up of different species of birds can be observed foraging together. Flocking together allows the birds to find more food and be more alert to danger. The birds all need to consume the same scarce resources, though. What two behaviors do these mixed flocks display?

   A competition and commensalism

   B mutualism and competition

   C parasitism and mutualism

   D predation and commensalism

14 Energy and matter move through and between organisms and the physical environment in the carbon cycle. This diagram shows part of the carbon cycle.

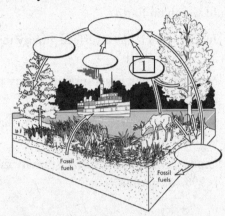

The process labeled "1" on the diagram indicates carbon moving from the deer into the atmosphere. What is happening in this process?

F The deer breaks down sugars and releases carbon dioxide.

G The deer converts carbon dioxide into sugars.

H The deer decomposes and absorbs carbon.

I The deer releases energy and stores carbon.

15 When Charles Darwin observed finches on the Galapagos Islands; he noted differences in the shapes of birds' beaks.

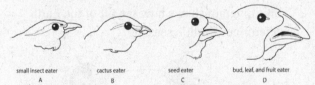

small insect eater A   cactus eater B   seed eater C   bud, leaf, and fruit eater D

If there is a two year drought that kills off many seed and fruit plants, which finch species have traits that could make them more successful?

A A and B

B A and C

C B and C

D C and D

16 Transitional fossils are fossils that help fill in gaps in the fossil record. One example of a transitional fossil is *Tiktaalik roseae*. It looks like a cross between a fish and a land animal. Which **best** describes what this organism is an example of?

F an organism that is still alive today

G evidence that organisms change over time

H evidence that organisms do not change over time

I evidence that life originated on land

17 In mice, the dominant *T* allele is responsible for brown fur, while the recessive *t* allele is responsible for white fur.

	?	?
T	*TT*	*TT*
t	*Tt*	*Tt*

If the parent genotype on the left is *Tt,* what is the parent genotype on the right?

A *tt*

B *Tp*

C *Tt*

D *TT*

18 Organisms are able to reproduce in different ways. Some are able to reproduce sexually, asexually, or both. Which is an advantage of sexual reproduction?

F quick

G does not need a partner

H produces genetic variation

I all offspring, not just females are able to produce offspring

19 Wyatt is making a model of our solar system. He is labeling the planets as terrestrial planets and gas giants. Which planet should he label as a terrestrial planet?

A Jupiter

B Neptune

C Uranus

D Venus

20 Space exploration has advanced our knowledge of the universe. Which space journey would take the longest?

F a journey from Earth to a star in the constellation Centaurus

G a journey from Earth to the farthest planet in our solar system, Neptune

H a journey from Earth to the moon

I a journey from Earth to the sun

21 Maya is at the observatory examining a newly discovered star through a powerful telescope. She wants to find out how bright the star actually is. What information will help her calculate the absolute magnitude of the star?

A color of the star

B composition of the star

C distance from Earth to the star

D temperature of the star

22 An atmosphere acts as insulation to keep a planet's surface warm. Mercury has almost no atmosphere. How does the lack of atmosphere affect temperatures on Mercury?

F Temperatures vary less than they would if Mercury had an atmosphere.

G Temperatures vary more than they would if Mercury had an atmosphere.

H Temperatures would be affected only when Mercury is closest to the sun.

I Temperatures would not be affected if Mercury had an atmosphere.

23 Weight depends on the force of gravity. The greater the gravitational attraction of a planet, the more an object weighs on that planet. On which planet would you weigh less than you would weigh on Earth?

A Jupiter, which has a surface gravity that is 253% of Earth's

B Neptune, which has a surface gravity that is 112% of Earth's

C Saturn, which has a surface gravity that is 106% of Earth's

D Uranus, which has a surface gravity that is 79% of Earth's

24 Based on the information in the table, which star **most likely** has the highest surface temperature?

Star	Color
Canopus	yellowish-white
Alpha Centauri	yellow-orange
Arcturus	Orange
Vega	bluish-white

F Alpha Centauri

G Arcturus

H Canopus

I Vega

25 This diagram shows how the tilt of the Earth determines Earth's seasons.

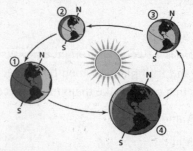

What season is the Northern Hemisphere experiencing in location 3?

A winter

B spring

C summer

D fall

26 Eclipses are predictable solar system events. Which list represents the position of Earth, the sun, and the moon during a solar eclipse?

F   Earth, sun, moon

G   moon, sun, Earth

H   sun, Earth, moon

I   sun, moon, Earth

27 What type of plate boundary is shown here?

A   convection

B   convergent

C   divergent

D   transform

28 Sediments from mountains many miles away are now in the area known as Florida. Which is the **best** explanation as to how most of these sediments moved so far away from where the mountains are now?

F   Rocks form more small, easily transported sediment on the southern side of mountains.

G   This range of mountains used to be much farther south than it is now.

H   The sediments were transported and deposited by streams and rivers.

I   The wind blew the sediments there.

29 A team of geologists compared the rock layers found in Florida to those found in northwest Africa. They placed all of the rock layers from the two regions in order from youngest to oldest. What did the team make?

A   a fossil reference

B   a geologic column

C   a geologic record

D   a topographic map

30 Fossils can be used to determine the relative ages of rock layers. Where will fossils of a more recent organism be located in undisturbed rock layers?

F   the deepest layer

G   always above the ground

H   above rock containing fossils of older organisms

I   below rock containing fossils of older organisms

31 Imagine you could travel in a straight line through Earth from a point on one side and come out on the other side. Which compositional layer would you travel through in the exact center of Earth?

A   core

B   crust

C   lithosphere

D   mantle

32 Which is **not** true about how the locations of volcanoes relate to tectonic plate boundaries?

F   Composite volcanoes are most common along convergent plate boundaries.

G   Most fissure eruptions occur at divergent plate boundaries.

H   The formation of volcanoes is not related to plate tectonics.

I   Volcanoes can also occur away from plate boundaries at hot spots.

33 The continent of Antarctica is covered with an ice sheet. Which part of Earth includes the ice sheet?

A   atmosphere

B   biosphere

C   cryosphere

D   hydrosphere

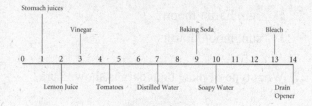

34 What is this map of Florida showing?

FLORIDA RAINFALL

ALABAMA GEORGIA 80°W

Jacksonville

St. Augustine

LEGEND
Average Yearly
Rainfall
Inches
60–80
50–60
40–50

Gulf of
Mexico

Orlando

FLORIDA

ATLANTIC
OCEAN

N
W   E
S

Miami

km 0   50   100
mi 0   50   100

25°N

85°W   80°W

F climate: average annual rainfall in Florida

G climate: rainfall for one day in Florida

H weather: average annual rainfall in Florida

I weather: rainfall for one day in Florida

35 The sun transmits energy to Earth, which is absorbed by the geosphere. This energy transfers to the atmosphere. The warm air rises and is pushed upward and outward by cooler air sinking. Which **best** describes these processes?

A conduction and convection

B radiation and conduction

C radiation and convection

D radiation, conduction, and convection

36 Density is the ratio of mass to volume. Devon recorded the density of four metals at a temperature of 20 °C.

Material	Density (g/cm^3)
brass	8.9
gold	19.3
iron	7.8
lead	11.3

If Devon has a 4 cm cube of each of these metals, which cube will have the **greatest** mass?

F brass

G gold

H iron

I lead

37 Some mixtures are classified as acids or bases. The pH scale shows how acidic or how basic these compounds are. Vinegar, a common cleaning agent, has a pH of about 2.2.

pH Values of Common Substances

Stomach juices

Vinegar

Baking Soda

Bleach

0 1 2 3 4 5 6 7 8 9 10 11 12 13 14

Lemon Juice   Tomatoes   Distilled Water   Soapy Water   Drain Opener

Which phrase describes vinegar?

A highly acidic

B highly basic

C slightly acidic

D slightly basic

38 Which **best** describes the composition of a solid?

F Particles are able to move freely.

G Particles are close together and able to move some.

H Particles at the top of the solid are tightly packed while particles at the bottom are very loose.

I Particles are tightly packed together, and are not able to move much.

39 Atoms of different elements can join together in arrangements to produce a variety of substances that are found on Earth. There are more than a hundred known elements. Which **best** describes these elements?

A Most of these elements are metalloids.

B Most of these elements are metals.

C Most of these elements are noble gases.

D Most of these elements are nonmetals.

40 All matter has both physical and chemical properties. A physical property can be observed without changing the identity of the substance. Which is a physical property?

F ability to rust

G density

H flammability

I reactivity with water

41 Sofie put a log with a mass of 5 kg on the campfire. After burning, the mass of the ash is 1 kg. Which **best** explains what may have happened to the other 4 kg?

A The other 4 kg disappeared.

B The other 4 kg turned into another log.

C The other 4 kg turned into liquid and seeped into the ground.

D The other 4 kg was released as gases.

42 What are the highest-frequency and lowest-frequency parts of the EM spectrum?

F Gamma rays are the lowest-frequency, and radio waves are the high frequency.

G Microwaves are the lowest-frequency, and x-rays are the highest-frequency.

H Radio waves are the lowest-frequency, and gamma rays are the highest frequency.

I X-rays are the lowest-frequency, and microwaves are the highest-frequency.

43 What is white light?

A a combination of green and red light

B a combination of red and blue light

C a combination of red, green, and blue light

D a lack of light

44 Mechanical waves travel as disturbances in a physical medium. How do electromagnetic waves travel?

F They cannot travel in a medium.

G They must travel in a liquid.

H They must travel in a solid.

I They travel as disturbances in electric and magnetic fields.

45 This diagram shows a flashlight shining light on a surface. Then the light bounces off at an angle.

Which **best** describes this?

A absorption

B reflection

C refraction

D scattering

46 Toasting bread in a toaster requires energy transformations.

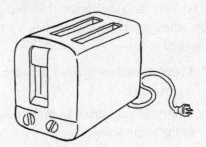

Which energy transformations occur in a toaster?

F chemical to thermal

G electrical to thermal

H mechanical to thermal

I thermal to chemical

47 As the skier glides down the mountain, energy is transformed.

Which **best** describes the transformation of energy happening in this diagram?

A The skier has kinetic energy at the top of the hill, and as he skis down, he loses energy.

B The skier has no energy at the top of the hill, and as he skis down the hill, he makes kinetic energy.

C The skier has the most kinetic energy at the top of the hill, and as he skis down the hill, kinetic energy transforms into potential energy.

D The skier has the most potential energy at the top of the hill, and as he skis down the hill, potential energy transforms into kinetic energy.

48 Which describes the correct direction of heat flow when you place ice cubes in a warm glass of water?

F Energy is not transferred from the ice to the warm water.

G Energy is transferred from the cold ice cubes to the warm water.

H Energy is transferred from the outside of the glass to the warm water.

I Energy is transferred from the warm water to the cold ice cubes.

49 A student is measuring the force required to move an object. Which of the forces shown in the diagram is a noncontact force?

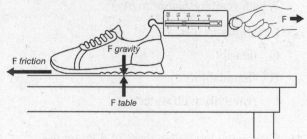

A the force of friction

B the force of gravity

C the force of the student's pull

D the force of the table

50 Two forces are applied on a soccer ball. Which explains why the ball accelerates?

F A net force applied to the ball is 0 N.

G Newton's second law does not apply to round objects.

H The ball resists one force but not the other.

I The two forces are unbalanced.

51 Samantha places a ball at the top of a hill, and the ball begins to roll down the hill. Which pair of forces is unbalanced?

A friction and air resistance

B gravity and acceleration

C net force and the normal force

D friction and gravity

52 This graph shows a variety of moving objects and how their distance is related to time.

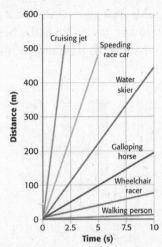

What do these objects have in common?

F They are all accelerating.

G They are all decelerating.

H They are all going the same speed.

I They are all moving at a constant speed.

53 Dr. Rashad performed an experiment to test whether she could cure a dangerous disease in mice. She found that her cure worked. Other scientists did not accept Dr. Rashad's findings right away because they had not yet been replicated. Which **best** describes why replication is important?

A Replication allows more mice to be cured of the disease.

B Replication can show if there were any errors in the research.

C Replication gives more scientists the opportunity to work.

D Replication would not give Dr. Rashad data to support her claim.

54 A class of thirty students was investigating whether temperature affects how quickly substances dissolve in water. The students formed groups of three and performed an experiment. The table shows steps the students took in their investigation.

Experimental Steps	
1	Put 100 mL of 20 °C distilled water into a beaker.
2	Put 100 mL of 40 °C distilled water into a beaker.
3	Pour 100 g of sugar into each beaker, note the time
4	Stir water once every 3 seconds
5	Record the time when no more sugar crystals are visible in each beaker.

Which **best** describes how the students validated results from their experiment?

F They used independent variables by adding sugar and distilled water.

G They used independent variables by recording temperatures and times.

H They used repetition by having multiple groups run the same trial.

I They used replication by having multiple groups run the same trial.

55 Scientists, such as biologists and physicists, study different topics. Which choice describes a way in which all scientists act similarly?

A All scientists ask questions about how life on Earth is possible.

B All scientists ask questions and use evidence to answer them.

C All scientists need to receive the same levels of education.

D All scientists use similar tools when doing investigations.

56 Scientists make models to help explain things that are difficult or impossible to observe directly. Scientists have revised the model of the atom numerous times. The image shows several scientific models of the atom.

Thomson's model of atom   Rutherford's model of atom   Current model of atom

Why would scientists **most likely** revise a scientific model?

F Advances in science can show how older models are flawed.

G Newer models tend to look more appealing than older models.

H Older models tend to be less informative than newer models.

I Old technology did not allow scientists to accurately measure.

57 Isaac Newton's law of universal gravitation provides an equation for calculating the force of gravity on an object. Einstein's theory of general relativity explains the observations of the forces of gravity as well as other evidence about how gravity, space, and time are related. What is the main difference between a law and a theory?

A A law is an explanation of many facts, a theory is an untested hypothesis.

B A law is one tested hypothesis, a theory is a collection of tested hypotheses.

C A law is a statement of a scientific fact, a theory is an explanation of many facts.

D A law is a rule about how science should be studied, a theory is an untested hypothesis.

58 The diagram shows the scientific idea which relates the pressure of a gas to its volume. Applying this idea gives scientists a ratio they can apply to any gas. What is the **best** way to describe what the diagram represents?

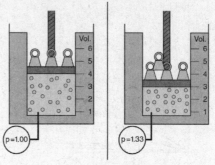

$pV = C$

F The diagram represents a hypothesis because it needs to be tested.

G The diagram represents a law because it shows a relationship that always applies.

H The diagram represents an experiment because it shows an idea being tested.

I The diagram represents a theory because it explains many observations.

59 Jenvieve just concluded an experiment. Her results do not support her hypothesis. Is her hypothesis worthless?

A Most likely, a hypothesis cannot be changed, so the hypothesis and experiment have no value.

B No, a hypothesis cannot be changed; therefore an experiment that is not be supported by data is not valuable.

C Not necessarily, the hypothesis is valuable if it leads to further investigation, even if it is not supported by data.

D Yes, a hypothesis that is not supported is not valuable.

60 The table shows the data collected during an experiment about plant height.

Plant	Amount of Water Given	Amount of Fertilizer Given	Height
1	10 mL	none	6 cm
2	20 mL	5 g	8 cm
3	30 mL	10 g	7 cm
4	40 mL	15 g	12 cm

How would you alter this experiment to investigate how water affects optimal growth of a plant?

F I would have fertilizer be the independent variable.

G I would have water and fertilizer both be independent variables.

H I would have water be the independent variable.

I I would have water be the dependent variable.

Name _____ Date _____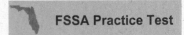

PLEASE NOTE	**Practice Test**

Mark one answer for each question.

- Use only a no. 2 pencil.
- Example:
- Erase changes COMPLETELY.

1 Ⓐ Ⓑ Ⓒ Ⓓ 21 Ⓐ Ⓑ Ⓒ Ⓓ 41 Ⓐ Ⓑ Ⓒ Ⓓ

2 Ⓕ Ⓖ Ⓗ Ⓘ 22 Ⓕ Ⓖ Ⓗ Ⓘ 42 Ⓕ Ⓖ Ⓗ Ⓘ

3 Ⓐ Ⓑ Ⓒ Ⓓ 23 Ⓐ Ⓑ Ⓒ Ⓓ 43 Ⓐ Ⓑ Ⓒ Ⓓ

4 Ⓕ Ⓖ Ⓗ Ⓘ 24 Ⓕ Ⓖ Ⓗ Ⓘ 44 Ⓕ Ⓖ Ⓗ Ⓘ

5 Ⓐ Ⓑ Ⓒ Ⓓ 25 Ⓐ Ⓑ Ⓒ Ⓓ 45 Ⓐ Ⓑ Ⓒ Ⓓ

6 Ⓕ Ⓖ Ⓗ Ⓘ 26 Ⓕ Ⓖ Ⓗ Ⓘ 46 Ⓕ Ⓖ Ⓗ Ⓘ

7 Ⓐ Ⓑ Ⓒ Ⓓ 27 Ⓐ Ⓑ Ⓒ Ⓓ 47 Ⓐ Ⓑ Ⓒ Ⓓ

8 Ⓕ Ⓖ Ⓗ Ⓘ 28 Ⓕ Ⓖ Ⓗ Ⓘ 48 Ⓕ Ⓖ Ⓗ Ⓘ

9 Ⓐ Ⓑ Ⓒ Ⓓ 29 Ⓐ Ⓑ Ⓒ Ⓓ 49 Ⓐ Ⓑ Ⓒ Ⓓ

10 Ⓕ Ⓖ Ⓗ Ⓘ 30 Ⓕ Ⓖ Ⓗ Ⓘ 50 Ⓕ Ⓖ Ⓗ Ⓘ

11 Ⓐ Ⓑ Ⓒ Ⓓ 31 Ⓐ Ⓑ Ⓒ Ⓓ 51 Ⓐ Ⓑ Ⓒ Ⓓ

12 Ⓕ Ⓖ Ⓗ Ⓘ 32 Ⓕ Ⓖ Ⓗ Ⓘ 52 Ⓕ Ⓖ Ⓗ Ⓘ

13 Ⓐ Ⓑ Ⓒ Ⓓ 33 Ⓐ Ⓑ Ⓒ Ⓓ 53 Ⓐ Ⓑ Ⓒ Ⓓ

14 Ⓕ Ⓖ Ⓗ Ⓘ 34 Ⓕ Ⓖ Ⓗ Ⓘ 54 Ⓕ Ⓖ Ⓗ Ⓘ

15 Ⓐ Ⓑ Ⓒ Ⓓ 35 Ⓐ Ⓑ Ⓒ Ⓓ 55 Ⓐ Ⓑ Ⓒ Ⓓ

16 Ⓕ Ⓖ Ⓗ Ⓘ 36 Ⓕ Ⓖ Ⓗ Ⓘ 56 Ⓕ Ⓖ Ⓗ Ⓘ

17 Ⓐ Ⓑ Ⓒ Ⓓ 37 Ⓐ Ⓑ Ⓒ Ⓓ 57 Ⓐ Ⓑ Ⓒ Ⓓ

18 Ⓕ Ⓖ Ⓗ Ⓘ 38 Ⓕ Ⓖ Ⓗ Ⓘ 58 Ⓕ Ⓖ Ⓗ Ⓘ

19 Ⓐ Ⓑ Ⓒ Ⓓ 39 Ⓐ Ⓑ Ⓒ Ⓓ 59 Ⓐ Ⓑ Ⓒ Ⓓ

20 Ⓕ Ⓖ Ⓗ Ⓘ 40 Ⓕ Ⓖ Ⓗ Ⓘ 60 Ⓕ Ⓖ Ⓗ Ⓘ